Polter

CW00665124

A New Exploration of Poltergeist Phenomena

(Short Stories From Hogwarts of Power and Pesky Poltergeists)

Edward Wallen

Published By **Ryan Princeton**

Edward Wallen

Poltergeist: A New Exploration of Poltergeist Phenomena (Short Stories From Hogwarts of Power and Pesky Poltergeists)

ISBN   978-1-998927-88-3

No part of this guidebook shall be reproduced in any form without permission in writing from the publisher except in the case of brief quotations embodied in critical articles or reviews.

Legal & Disclaimer

Table Of Contents

Chapter 1: What Are The Poltergeist Phenomena?

Typically, the poltergeist manifestations involve recurrence of one or more of the subsequent phenomena

(Apparently paranormal)

•Start or bombarding projectiles (eg. Stones or unique small devices)

•Opening, final or slamming doors or home windows

•Movements (along side levitation) family gadgets (furniture, glass ...)

•Sounds or crackles

•imitative sounds (the sound of a crying little one or a barking dog ...)

•Puddles, floods

•Outbreaks of hearth

•Pinching, biting or scratching the pores and pores and skin

•Graffiti or written (on the partitions ...)

•Electrical disturbances and mechanical failures.

•Lights or slight effects.

Significantly, pretty a few those activities are commonplace to trendy and historic poltergeists instances, suggesting that there may be a everyday model of the phenomena involved.

However, the huge majority of registered instances of poltergeists have been held in Europe or America.

Representation a poltergeist. 1911

The poltergeist agent

The poltergeist instances are commonly domestic affairs, with the phenomena affecting especially the house and the right away family.

Sometimes the place of business is involved.

Typically, a member of the family appears to be the middle of poltergeist interest, that individual is gift whilst the sports get up, and looks one way or a few other motive their occurrence.

Unlike the case of obsessions, which can be commonly related to precise places, poltergeist cases seem to cognizance on a particular character (every now and then).

When the family moved to the house, the phenomena now and again observe that individual (called "poltergeist agent")

The poltergeist agent is usually a infant, adolescent, or more younger character - typically a pre-pubescent girl (nine-thirteen years).

In many times poltergeist, there are complicated and emotionally conflicting own family dynamics.

Often, the family has a strict regime, authoritarian and punitive, and may be particularly spiritual.

A broadly normal principle is that the poltergeist phenomena are a manifestation of psychokinetic immoderate anger of the agent to some other family member

(Which also can, at once or in a roundabout way, be the target of the hobby).

Often, anger seems to be directed simply so the poltergeist agent becomes the victim.

Despite the regularly dramatic and threatening nature of the events, humans centered are rarely injured by way of using way of phenomena.

Physical harm is normally restricted to scratches, minor cuts or bruises small, sometimes due to photographs.

Levitation chairs

Outbreaks of Poltergeist

Poltergeist times unexpectedly erupt, regularly caused through a disturbing occasion, or a brand new supply of emotional strain.

Most outbreaks do no longer very last some of weeks or months, and generally stop all at once.

Some wonderful instances, however, endured for numerous years.

Often, the pastime disappears at the equal time as there can be a huge trade in the person and circle of relatives situations (moving, changing schools or exchange in the composition of the household).

The man or woman or own family counseling or psychotherapy also can assist to cease the epidemic.

Poltergeists and deception

Skeptics argue that many, if no longer all, poltergeist times are the cease end result of deception - typically via the poltergeist agent, sometimes with accomplices.

They issue out that the agent is often a young infant or teenager who honestly makes jokes, both for a laugh or mischief, or to draw attention, or to explicit a repressed hostility or exacting revenge toward a hated person, family member.

In a minority of times, the poltergeist sellers have been stuck within the act (eg starting or shifting gadgets).

Although no longer regularly determined, skeptics advocate that certain trends of poltergeist cases recommend that the fraud can be an awful lot extra large than it seems.

This includes the truth that observers almost normally see already flying projectiles, they do no longer see the object to begin its movement.

Other sports (imitative sounds, graffiti ...) are very easy to imitate, while the most dramatic phenomena (levitation) are uncommon and notoriously difficult to report.

It is likewise vital to understand that a few deception can be unconscious, in all likelihood made in a dissociated intellectual u . S . A ., instead of a planned act of mischief or revenge.

Such unconscious deception can also certainly be an critical clue to help us recognize the psychological foundations of a poltergeist case.

Theories Poltergeists

If the fraud is excluded, there are four vital theories which have been advanced to offer an motive behind the poltergeist manifestations:

Natural motives

In some instances, the phenomena can be described as a misinterpretation of natural activities.

For example, the noises inside the partitions or cavities of a residence may be because of birds or rodents.

The noise and vibration can also be because of wind, underground streams, to fasten within the plumbing or earthquakes.

Puddles and flooding can end result from leaks or condensation.

Estimates advocate, however, that herbal artifacts constitute a very small percent of poltergeist phenomena said (a whole lot much less than 2%).

Explanations spiritualists

The conventional belief structures normally count on that the phenomena are due to mischievous or evil spirits, ghosts, or demons.

In some instances, it is concept that these religious entities have the sufferer.

poltergeist activities are consequently confronted with fear, and with attempts to non secular or magical treatments regarding ritual, prayer, or exorcism.

With the advent of Spiritualism movement within the 1840s, the protests have been understood as attempts with the resource of the departed souls to speak with the dwelling, perhaps if you need to remedy unfinished agency and be unfastened from kingdom earthly.

The spiritualist technique poltergeists, consequently, is generally to installation a communique channel with the departed soul with the aid of using organizing a mediumship consultation.

In these meetings, the "poltergeist" (thoughts) can reputedly show his identification with the useful useful resource of using a coded device or thru using voice phenomena, or in writing, or the usage of a ouija board.

Interestingly, individuals who later come to be spiritualist mediums are frequently the middle of a poltergeist interest in their early life.

Psychokinetic motives

Psychokinesis refers to the obvious functionality of some people to use highbrow powers.

Because the phenomena commonly tend to interest at some stage in the poltergeist agent, it's miles counseled that they will be due to spontaneous eruptions of latent psychokinetic powers of the agent.

As poltergeist outbreaks are normally associated with excessive stages of emotional strain, it is also assumed that this may expand the psychokinetic electricity till they in the end explode as a poltergeist interest.

It emerge as also cautioned that environmental elements can enlarge the psychokinetic power in effective willing humans, most important to poltergeist manifestations.

In precise, research suggests an association with electromagnetic fields (proximity to excessive voltage power strains) or geomagnetic disturbances (due to sun hobby).

Psychological and psychiatric reasons

Psychological and psychiatric factors seem to play an vital function in most instances of poltergeist, often contributing to the stress experienced.

Most poltergeist dealers are young children or teens who also can conflict to cope with the onset of puberty, with circle of relatives tensions and different interpersonal troubles, or with bodily, verbal or sexual.

In in many instances, the emergence of poltergeist is preceded through an identifiable emotional or interpersonal catastrophe.

In some times, the character may be recognized with an anxiety illness, a hysterical conversion or dissociative circumstance.

Multiple personality has additionally been suggested as a element in some instances.

The intellectual, psychiatric and psychosocial factors virtually play an vital characteristic inside the protests.

They can help give an explanation for what triggers and keeps a pandemic, they also can advise a motivation for cheating.

But they can not provide an cause in the back of a surely paranormal activity.

If factors of a poltergeist instances are presumed to be paranormal, a absolutely psychological and psychiatric interpretation need to be complemented through a angle that acknowledges the para-ordinary phenomena.

Chapter 2: Investigate And Examine Instances Of Poltergeist

By their nature, poltergeist times are complicated, hard and now and again traumatic.

Investigators normally face masses of realistic troubles, interpersonal and moral, and frequently discover that phenomena are beyond their direct commentary and recording attempts.

The essential proof in lots of instances based on the testimony of witnesses whose memories aren't normally apparent and reliable or constant.

It can be hard to get a definitive opinion at the question of whether or now not a poltergeist case absolutely indicates paranormal occasions, or activities can be described with the aid of deception or different herbal reasons.

The paranormal hobby can be excluded past much less steeply-priced doubt.

Clear evidence of hoax, an unambiguous confession, or an potential to offer an reason for all phenomena through the use of herbal reasons.

The paranormal interest is viable but now not going.

There are important problems with proof (Lack of impartial witnesses, insufficient studies, or sizeable warning signs of hoax or natural reasons).

The paranormal hobby seems possible.

The phenomena are decided through the usage of independent witnesses.

Standard honest studies.

Natural reasons aren't going.

A few minor pointers may be determined.

The paranormal hobby seems probably.

Phenomena decided via using numerous impartial witnesses or recording device, specific degree of investigation.

Natural motives are not going.

The paranormal interest is strongly indicated.

whole evidence of severa credible impartial witnesses or recording machine.

If cautiously studied.

No proof of cheating observed.

The phenomena can not be described with the useful useful resource of natural reasons.

The paranormal activity is mounted past low-cost doubt.

Indisputable proof of paranormal phenomena without deception warning signs and signs and symptoms.

The phenomenon is big in all nations of the arena, in the islands, in short, on all continents.It is also present in every age.

The researcher Hereward Carrington has identified five preceding to the 12 months 1000, one hundred and thirty, among the eleventh century and the overdue nineteenth century.

Germany

Poltergeist Bigen

858 AD

Found inside the "ringed Fulda" one of the oldest regarded rapper mentions mind.

The chronicle opinions that during 858 AD, on a farm in Bingen at the Rhine, an "evil spirit" threw stones and shook the partitions as though they have been hit with a hammer.

stones jets are one of the favored activities of

poltergeist.

View of the present day-day city of Bingen, which came about on poltergeis

Poltergeist Rosenheim

1967

The maximum well-known example is probably studied with the beneficial resource of Hans Bender (professor at Freiburg, Germany), called the

"Rosenheim poltergeist."

Here's the story, taken from Broughton

On a cold morning in November 1967 maximum of the felony expert Sigmund Adam staff had been already at paintings in his have a study of the Bavarian town of Rosenheim.

One of the remaining humans to attain become Anne-Marie Schneider, a secretary of eighteen years currently employed.

Anne-Marie Schneider aged 19, definitely employed as a secretary.

She entered the hall and took off his coat.

As she surpassed under a placing lamp, it began to sway, however the female did now not be conscious the phenomenon.

She walked to the locker room, and the motion of the lamp grew louder.

Suddenly the mild bulb of the locker room started out out to sway too.

An worker who had monitored his get right of entry to gave him:

"Achtung! Lamp Die ! "

Anne-Marie bent and pulled his coat for protection.

A second later, the mild inside the hall exploded, sending a rain of glass shards within the direction of Anne-Marie.

The swinging of the wire ceased, and with a few terms of manner to the worker who had warned, Anne-Marie took a brush to pick out up the glass.

The special officers plunged anew into their art work.

They had been used now.

However the attorney grow to be a concerned damage.

His place of business have turn out to be gift method a quick self-destruction and his commercial enterprise slowed drastically.

Fluorescent tubes related to the ceiling continuously falling down.

Once he finished a loud bang and all of the lighting fixtures went out . When the electrician, climbed the ladder, examined neon tubes, he noticed that that they had became ninety levels of their homes, interrupting the electric connection.

No quicker had he again all in walking order some other loud bang modified into heard and that each one the lights went out another time.

Even when they have been now not lit, incandescent bulbs exploded without the filament is damaged.

The seals were jumping for no obvious reason, and on occasion on my own éjectaient their homes. The smartphone malfunctions have been particularly crucial.

The four blended sounded simultaneously with out there has been none on the alternative end. Telephone conversations have been often interrupted for quick periods, or reduce altogether.

The cellphone payments reached aberrant amounts, and sort of known as numbers were never charged.

The growing liquid in the photocopying machines, frequently flowed from the reservoir without the device have emerge as touched.

First, Adam and personnel suspected disabilities electric powered system.

Engineers from the municipal strength station and the publish place of business (who treated the cellphone gadget) were called and monitoring tool installed on electricity traces to discover any alternate of waft depth.

These devices enregistrèrent very large waft fluctuations, which regularly coincide with the discovered phenomena.

It déconnecta examine of municipal electricity deliver and battery backup have become added in advance than presenting modern-day without disruption.

The contemporary intensity variations and phenomena persisted.

Recording devices have been additionally connected to the phones to maintain song of the entirety from name workplaces.

Almost as speedy as they function, they recorded calls sent workplace whilst no one changed into the use of the mobile phone.

The recordings discovered a great shape of calls to the speaking clock (which in Germany isn't always a free employer), regularly six consistent with minute.

On 20 October, forty-six calls to the talking clock in fifteen mins had been recorded.

Professor Hans Bender of the University of Friborg, senior investigator for poltergeists, arrived with a few colleagues December 1.

A week later, they had been joined thru two physicists on the Max Planck Institute specialists in plasma physics, F. Karger and G. Zicha, who started out out to look for abnormalities in the electric powered powered

and cellular cellphone tool.

F. Karger and G. Zicha

Bender's group speedy located unexplained phenomena and strength disturbances are produced only at some point of walking hours.

He moreover have grow to be brief obvious that every one the ones phenomena needed to middle the person of Anne-Marie.

Often, the primary anomaly recorded via the monitoring device took place at the same time as Anne-Marie crossed the edge of the workplace within the morning.

 Bender assumed it become a case of RSPK that the girl modified into the agent.

Upon arrival, Karger and Zicha undertook to test the assets of power.

On December eight, they adjoignirent extra machine to the ones already in area.

Between 16 and 17 h 30 h 48 that day, the tool recorded fifteen sudden float variations at regular periods.

At approximately the identical time, very loud creaking have become heard, similar to those that could have produced big sparks, even though each electric alternate turn out to be now not positioned systematically those sound activities.

All the sounds have been recorded on a tape recorder.

We even added the gadgets to diploma the electric potential and the magnetic area near the loggers and the noise amplitude in places of work.

Based on their research, the physicists judged they might cast off as achievable reasons variations in the electricity deliver, excessive frequency voltages demodulated, electrostatic expenses, outside static magnetic fields, ultrasonic or infra-sonic effects (which encompass vibration), defective connections or malfunctions recording devices and ultimately, manual intervention.

When Bender had explained his belief that disruptions had been because of PK, poltergeist hobby intensified.

Bender The institution and the engineers of the strength business enterprise and the law enforcement officials noticed the ornamental plates jump partitions and tables to swing or even turn round their tie hook.

Bender captured on videotape lamps swaying and detonation noises, but couldn't document the moves of tables.

Chapter 3: Company Photo Lamps Swaying

Another investigator the usage of their gadget, should record a table performing a rotation of 320 ranges on its axis.

The Freiburg team watched drawers establishing of themselves and documents which moved by myself.

Some drawers éjectèrent actually furniture.

Twice a 100 fifty pounds of workbook far from the wall approximately thirty centimeters. While the ones sports have been happening, the investigators said that Anne-Marie come to be increasingly fearful.

Finally she confirmed hysterical twitching of the legs and arms.

When she went to take a rest, the phenomena ceased right now.

Shortly after she positioned employment elsewhere, and the legal expert fine noted problem.

In offices in which Anne-Marie become now running some disruption happened, however a lot much less lovely and stopped time.

On more than thirty-five instances he studied, Professor Bender has constantly maintained that Rosenheim grow to be the maximum excellent.

This is the first-class documented case data on a "poltergeist"

If levitation

Mr. Adam, explaining the activities at the equal

time as a pen "levitates" with him

lamps oscillate

England

The drum Tedworth

1661

The drum Tedworth is one of the maximum famous poltergeist but the oldest registered in England one night time in March 1661, the own family of a Justice of the Peace, John Monpesson modified into wakened from his sleep with the useful resource of drumbeats who maintained conscious until dawn.

Some time in the past, Mompesson had arrested a drifter named William Drury, who roamed the streets drumming, and had confiscated his tool regardless of his protests.

Drury escaped, but his drum.

The nocturnal disturbances in Mompesson began out speedy after; they persisted for 2 years.

In addition to the drumbeats thoughts changed into slamming doors and bring all styles of noises:

gasps, hum, crackle ...

He also shouted:

" a witch ! A witch ! ".

poltergeist emptied the ashes and the contents of the pot chamber pots inside the beds, and whirled items all through the room.

In 1663, Drury became all over again imprisoned for robbery; he identified that it have become at the start issues, such as that he may hold as Mompesson no longer it may not have made his drum.

The demonstrations stopped after years.

00015.Gif

The Borley rectory

1862 /1944

The Borley rectory changed into an imposing Victorian brick constructing placed within the parish of Borley, in Essex, England.

Built in 1862 on the ruins of an vintage constructing destroyed via hearth in 1841, he had served as pastor stays Henry Bull and his circle of relatives.

That rectory taken into consideration cursed and dubbed "the most haunted house in England" emerge as destroyed through manner of fireplace at some level inside the Second World War and subsequently destroyed in 1944.

Despite this, his recognition is remembered ...

The Borley rectory turn out to be a big neo-Gothic fashion house constructed in 1862 in Borley (Essex County in England) to deal with the Rev. Henry Bull and his circle of relatives.

The presbytery modified into raised on a preceding constructing web page, a Cistercian monastery courting from the Middle Ages destroyed by means of fireside in 1841.

The Borley rectory is considered "the maximum haunted residence in England."

Destroyed via hearth within the path of World War II and demolished in 1944, it remains a mythical net website.

In truth, ghosts and poltergeists decided Borley rectory are the strangest. Haunting phenomena have been severa.

The Borley rectory is surrounded with the resource of outstanding anecdotes and recollections of paranormal phenomena positioned in the domestic.

But I want to provide you with a warning, high priced readers, this net page belongs extra to legend than data and it's far difficult to disentangle myth from fact.

Especially nowadays, the presbytery no longer exists and no research is feasible, but, its

history and the reminiscences are chilling.

Presbytery in 1939

A legend tells that the area of the presbytery, there was a Cistercian monastery built inside the Middle Ages which contained a suitable treasure guarded with the aid of manner of the priests.

It is idea that the treasure belonged to the Knights Templar got here to France after the dissolution of the Order in 1314.

Others think that the treasure will be the wealth accumulated with the aid of the priests.

This is why monks couldn't have left the scene and hang-out the presbytery.

They should keep to keep the treasure.

Another anecdote issues the Queen Mary. In 1568, she turn out to be defeated and compelled to abdicate.

She fled to her enemy Elizabeth of England along along with his private results. Thus the monastery treasure was found enriched the wealth of the kings of Scotland.

These riches were entrusted to the clergymen with the resource of the treasurer of the royal circle of relatives and it's miles said that the escort who accompanied him to the monastery to put the treasure modified into slaughtered to hold the call of the sport.

A extra sensible legend keeps that the whereabouts nocturnal, numerous issues of the apparitions ghosts and assaults through using evil entities that have been decided at the internet web page might actually be the impact of greed and horrible religion of the exceptional priests.

Indeed, the pirates have given treasures to the clergymen and they in no manner desired to make. They preferred to get rich. The hackers would possibly then murdered all the clergymen and burned the monastery.

Over the years, the place's reputation has traveled to England and became a reference for all hunters ghosts, Much similar to the Amityville house the united states besides that the Amityville house but exists these days.

The information of Borley Rectory can be very exciting. There become noted a large range (over 3000) of paranormal phenomena.

In addition, the well-known press become interested in him.

The media attracted many onlookers, mediums, lighting fixtures ... From across the arena to attend a supernatural phenomenon.

In the institution, there were furthermore many who peddled mythomaniacs tall recollections, who made sensational statements in order to entice hobby to themselves.

This is why it is very difficult to kind fact from fiction in this story.

It became during those investigations turn out to be born a legend recounting the love affair of a more youthful and extremely good nun kidnapped through a younger monk Monastery Borley.

Denounced by way of manner of the farmer wearing them, the lovers have been stuck even as looking to get to London.

The monk become hanged and the nun grow to be condemned to be walled up alive within the crypt of the chapel.

In the Middle Ages, we do now not giggle with this stuff! Since then, the two fanatics avenge the use of away the populace of the presbytery.

Another legend speaks of a French nun, Marie Lairre, who after leaving the convent of Le Havre should have married a nobleman Borley, One Henry Waldregrave.

The Lord could have strangled his partner in 1667 inside the former monastery, inside the place wherein may be built later than Borley rectory.

The younger girl might in no manner have left the region and may be enamored of revenge.

This story originates from the account of seance done inside the constructing via the medium Helen Glanville.

This vicinity deemed cursed includes many distinct memories to delight horror.

Here are a few :

Some speak of a rider, a messenger from the Queen, who died eaten with the useful resource of foxes and rats having had four severed limbs and left at the roadside in pain.

There is also communicate of a clergyman, Father Enoch, who have become nailed alive by means of the use of bandits on the door of his oratory.

Supernatural events

With the improvement in 1863 of a current and blessed the building, the Reverend Henry Bull hoping to stop those legends and make his home a peaceful region.

But that did not take place as planned.

After a few months in the house, Henry Bull and his family started to see, pay interest, experience normal matters:

Dull blows from the basement or attic, blood oozing beams and ceiling footsteps night time, bells ringing, the appearances of entities ...

A 365 days after having moved one night, honestly one among Reverend's son complained of being slapped within the face with the beneficial aid of an invisible hand.

His little brother will whinge of being awoke at night via a person dressed with clothes of an antique time who's status through the mattress, armed and fixing it.

The partner of the Reverend have to have heard, three nights in a row, a team galloping down the aisle. She might have long past to check the window, however the courtyard changed into deserted.

Bull couple had 14 children and all have witnessed unexplainable phenomena.

These phenomena could even grow to be violent through the years:

Doors torn, damaged shutters, bizarre noises, pestilential smells, sounds terrifying, throwing stones on the roof, inexplicable motion of furnishings ...

The Reverend Henry Bull become a deeply religious guy. Given the significance of the occasions, he determined to attraction to the ecclesiastical authorities requesting an exorcism of places.

This request changed into conventional and an exorcist stood in Borley rectoryto easy infestations.

This exorcism restored peace within the residence for a while.

Bull kids attended the exorcism amazed.

The weeks that determined, they finished in the exorcist questioning no harm.

Several humans, who have visible them, claimed that paranormal phenomena taking location in the presbytery have been most effective kid's video games, children of Reverend had completed in ghosts and had enjoyed scaring the servants.

But this clarification did now not persuade the professionals of the paranormal.

The eldest son, Malcolm Bull, went to look at in Edinburgh to come to be Reverend like his father.

When he lower back, he took over from his father and settled in Borley rectory.

The latter married a fantastic Margaret and the couple had many kids, Harry and Jennifer.

The latter, bored at the rectory, performed to scare servants.

They disguised themselves as ghosts and at night time they roamed the rooms. Domestic spoke to the village and soon a rumor spread a number of the peasants:

the presbytery modified into haunted thru the Devil.

After World War II, Harry succeeded Malcolm. His ministry cherished a non violent duration. Harry knew the supernatural international and knew the manner to huntghosts and evil spirits.

More no supernatural manifestation came keep away from the tranquility of the residence.

In the early 20s, a rumor unfold within the village. Everywhere, it modified into said that the presbytery modified into haunted.

It want to be stated that during this period, numerous paranormal manifestations got here tarnish the popularity of the place.

Despite his understanding, Harry Bull couldn't save you them. The look is cited poltergeists, Night screams, rotting fruit in a unmarried night time, spoiled canned a virus of snakes, water wells poisoned ...

Villagers now not dared to visit Borley rectory, they whispered that the vicinity emerge as cursed and that reputation marred the Reverend.

Still, Harry Bull remained inside the house until his death in 1927, weakened and in poor fitness.

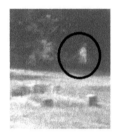

Chapter 4: The Ghost Of Borley

After the dying of Reverend Harry Bull, Eric Smith and his family moved to Borley rectory in 1928 irrespective of its awful reputation.

But Eric Smith did no longer agree with in those rumors.

Soon, the Smith own family changed into disturbed via regular occasions:

Mournful courtroom cases the night time time, footsteps, odd motion of devices and furnishings, and characteristic appearances ... Matters escalated brief.

There end up stone throwing, blood seeps into the partitions, the advent of slimy mushrooms inside the frames and beams. Mary Pearson, the residence of Smith, frightened, left the house.

She talked about maximum of those demonic manifestations to the villagers of Borley.

A reporter from the Daily Mirror have end up inquisitive about the rectory and posted an article June 10, 1929 in which he cited ghostly apparitions and diabolical signs and symptoms.

Therefore, the Borley rectory attracted many curious, Harry Price, a colourful man or woman, a pseudo-spiritualist, a fake medium, short a charlatan.

Rich and seductive, Harry Price declared himself "Hunter fantômes "And had based totally a" psychic National Laboratory Sciences ".

Harry Price went to Borley. He visited the presbytery, made a short research, interviewed villagers and decreed that the vicinity became fairly obsessed.

He persuaded Elder Smith to assist lead a greater thorough research.

The latter elegant.

Thus Harry Price lower decrease lower back to the parsonage discovered journalists on board a high-priced car, smoking a big cigar.

He drew interest to himself, bluffed residents Borley and rummaged unceremoniously into the intimate life of the latter. Do now not assisting all hype, Smith left the rectory.

The own family moved to Long Melford.

Rev. Smith despite the truth that continued to attend to his parish and its parishioners.

Curious flocked from at some stage in England. Eric Smith, not able to do more of these folks that located him all of the time, in the long run left the location and moved to Norfolk.

After his departure, the parsonage regained his composure for some months, until the arrival of Foyster own family.

The circle of relatives Foyster

Harry Price, Mollie Goldney and family Foyster

The Foyster arrived a few months after the departure of Smith. They settled on the rectory October 16, 1930.

Lionel Foyster, the patriarch, have turn out to be a cousin Harry Bull and knew the location for having spent his vacations.

With his spouse Marianne and their daughter Adelaide 2 years vintage, they took ownership. Lionel Foyster changed into a person rational that do not without hassle allow abuse, the presbytery's popularity did not frighten him.

But quickly the own family turned into disturbed through paranormal events:

Flood of pebbles, blood seeps into the walls, demonic entities appearances, howls and jeers of night and day ...

Sometimes the ones entities physical assaulted the hosts of the presbytery:

Scratches, bites, slaps ...

The servants have been even driven around in the large staircase of the house and crushed.

Lionel Foyster changed into once more called to Harry Price who got here to the area with tremendous fanfare decided this time to clear up the complete tale.

The first time, he couldn't prove the fact of supernatural activities.

When he arrived, he observed that the demonstrations have been even greater violent than the final. Satanic messages have been scrawled at the walls. Harry Price suspected

Marianne Foyster to have finished those messages, but could not accuse him overtly.

Moreover, this phenomenon persevered however the absence of Marianne inside the residence.

Harry Price, the self-proclaimed "hunter ghosts "Did no longer consider within the supernatural.

His purpose have become to expose that this entire element changed into the work of a prankster.

In January 1932, earlier than the activities and that can't deliver an explanation for, he determined to exorcise the presbytery through using manner of a set of spiritualists led by using Marks Tey, a désenvoûteur.

The latter modified into assisted via Guy L'Estrange, a medium.

The spiritualist organization effected prayers of purification and deliverance.

All supernatural manifestations ceased.

There had been greater than bizarre noises, more appearances, more stone throwing ...

But this lull did no longer last extended. Hardly the celebration organization that paranormal phenomena began out over again.

Strange song resounded through the church, the communion wine modified into converting frequently in ink, ladies and cows surrounding aborted without scientific cause, the hens stopped laying eggs, entities levitating all night time and were up perspectives 'village, it regarded that the extraordinary phenomena moreover affected at gift, the residents close by.

One morning, Marianne determined her daughter's face covered in blood. Her little body showed severa bruises. This have come to be too much for the mother who satisfied her husband to go away.

Thus in 1935, the left Foyster Borley eventually claiming to be pressured out and now not able to cope with the occasions.

After the departure of Foyster, the rectory changed into bought by using manner of way of the Church and became the Rev. Henning who settled it in 1936.

The latter might not live on the parsonage and requested permission to stay in Liston, a village near Borley.

In 1937, Harry Price rented the Borley rectory and came to settle there.

He had run an advert within the Times calling all healthful human beings in frame and thoughts to join their crew of witnesses for a year, day and night time time, Borley rectory.

The assertion additionally stated that each one scientists have been welcome, nominations were severa.

Price completed a number one preference and detained some Helen Glanville, expert Ouija, and kids as well as a diplomat with the aid of the call of Mark Kerr-Pearse.

The organization made, Price allotted the responsibilities to every of its employees and a guide describing strategies of investigation of a haunted vicinity.

Helen Glanville made some Ouija intervals and made startling revelations, together with that of Malcolm Barnes, a knight of the Queen of Scotland, useless unburied in Islam and can wander the moonlit nights searching out her sword studded gem stones who finds the treasure inside Borley.

Another revelation worried a few Lairre Marie, a nun murdered thru Henry Waldegrave. His mind ought to wander inside the rectory.

A consultation of Ouija taking location in March 1938 determined out the imminent destruction of the presbytery by using manner of hearth and the discovery within the ruins, the remains of a murdered nun.

And truly, those events passed off later ...

The destruction of the presbytery

The ruins of Borley Rectory after the fireside

William Gregson and his circle of relatives had been the final populace of the presbytery. Gregson come to be a rationalist skeptic.

He bought the home for a chunk of bread.

He had spoken with Harry Price (the latter, via the way, did no longer find any rational cause for paranormal activities).

William Gregson did now not accept as true with in anything, neither in God nor the devil or maybe less to the wandering souls.

However, as soon as installed, the spirits that inhabited the presbytery broke unfastened and the horrible man needed to face the statistics.

The supernatural worldwide existed.

Gregson had all of it:

Apparitions, blood on the walls, stone throwing, hitting, creepy noises, screams ...

During the night of 27 to twenty-eight February 1939, the rectory stuck fireside due to incorrect coping with of a kerosene lamp.

The residence stuck fireplace fast, the flames fast acquired upstairs.

The rectory modified into badly broken, uninhabitable. The fireside woke up the vintage legends.

Evil tongues asserted that the proprietors had burned the presbytery to get the insurance.

In 1943, Harry Price published his first ebook on the presbytery in which he associated his enjoy in locations.

The same three hundred and sixty 5 days, he resumed the research and searched the charred basements.

He determined a lady skeleton buried within the cellar.

He said it have become one of the nun expected with the aid of the Spirit that spoke through the Ouija board.

After the fireplace, the paranormal manifestations did no longer stop.

The spirits that haunted the parsonage have become moved to the church of BorleyOn the opportunity side of the road.

The media seized of the hassle again attracting a crowd of onlookers to Borley.

Professional and amateur photographers from time to time very enigmatic posted pix of some appearances.

These images have been normally rigged. Yet they had been taken very severely.

On a photograph, you can see a brick levitating in the air, at the possibility, an old guy hunched frame, the craggy face with out ears and no nostril.

Flying brick

A photographer Dick Gee showed a photograph taken inside the church on which we determined a halo of moderate in the middle.

It changed into idea that this appearance changed into an angel.

After World War II, Alan Gregson, a son of William Gregson, wrote a letter to his friend Richard Lee wherein he cited his youngsters recollections.

Richard Lee end up investigating the ghosts of the presbytery.

Alan counseled him what he had lived inside the rectory.

Richard Lee requested Richard Gregson, the little brother Alan, who stated the equal events in a extra dramatic version.

To have the coronary heart internet, Richard Lee requested Marianne Foyster who gave a detailed account of his memories and who claimed that all phenomena were exaggerated.

She introduced that she and her husband laughed the rantings they study within the newspapers about the rectory.

In 1958, Marianne Foyster confided to a group of researchers investigating the rectory.

For her, all of the occasions had been a staging.

She confessed that her husband, herself and her kids had all engineered, needed to do not forget in supernatural manifestations to make amusing of human beings's credulity.

She added that she had carved demonic inscriptions at the walls of the presbytery, mushrooms stuck some of the beams, used sparkling red meat blood to motive the famous seepage.

The concept of believing in a haunted vicinity came to him after an night with pals for the duration of which the vintage hostess had advised how she had loved in her teens into believing his mother and father that the house became haunted , with the aid of way of the use of dressing in ghost, throwing stones in opposition to the facade, hiding inside the attic, screaming, spreading stink ...

Chapter 5: The Poltergeist Enfield

1977/1980

Nothing on this balmy nighttime of August

seemed even slightly out of the everyday.

Peggy Hodgson have become busy storing the terrace of his residence in Enfield, north London, after her 4 youngsters have the unruly, another time, makes it seem like a pig ...

Mrs Hodgson's daughters have been getting ready to visit mattress upstairs.

As normal, Janet, eleven, finished his combat with Margaret older sister.

Then, as the two women laughed and rolled at the bed, something regular happened:

material wardrobe started to slowly drag them at the ground.

The sisters appeared horrified the fabric cloth cloth wardrobe at some point of the room as if it have been drawn through a couple of effective however invisible fingers.

They were even extra nervous after they located out that the okaycupboard could block the door of their room, their only way out.

Fortunately for the kids, the mom burst into the room to whinge approximately the noise.

She grabbed the cloth cupboard and driven towards the wall. But the invisible pressure continued.

Peggy, apprehensive, checked out the convenient begin to slide across the room.

This time, the furniture moved quicker and Peggy may additionally additionally need to do now not something to forestall it.

She tried to push the fabric cupboard in competition to the wall but couldn't.

And this time, she ought to revel in an inhumanly powerful stress within the room. Confused and terrified thru what she noticed, Peggy took her kids and fled the room panicked.

Thus commenced out one of the strangest instances of obsession ever recorded in England.

Over the following months, the phenomenon referred to as "Enfield poltergeist" chamboula the life of the Hodgson circle of relatives.

Toys, plates, cutlery, books and snap shots inexplicably flew throughout the room.

Objects seemed and miraculously disappeared earlier than the eyes of the terrified observers.

Such reminiscences might also appear truly absurd.

But what makes the case of Enfield so brilliant is that the sports had been thoroughly investigated with the resource of reliable instructors and, more pertinently, were seen with the beneficial useful resource of extra than 30 independent witnesses along with cops .

Although the obsession to be spent there 30 years, Janet and Margaret have not spoken publicly due to the fact youth.

They are despite the fact that reluctant to speak approximately the incident substantial as their life keeps.

But within the documentary Interview With A Poltergeist in March 2007, they broke his silence for the primary time and what they show sheds new moderate on one of the maximum superb paranormal incidents that has ever came about in England.

"I felt utilized by a stress that no man or woman is acquainted with," says Janet. "I truly do no longer need to remember it. I'm now not sure that the poltergeist become absolutely 'awful'. It turned into nearly as if he desired to be a part of our circle of relatives. He could not hurt us. He died there and wanted to rest in peace. The most effective manner he may additionally

need to talk turn out to be via me and my sister.
"

Hard skeptical put together dinner, of route, scoff at such pointers and declare that poltergeist testimonies are without a doubt the end stop end result of hoaxes and deceptions.

They cited that preadolescent are rarely dependable witnesses and, importantly, that Janet and her sister confessed to gambling recommendations on some of the ones despatched to research their obsession.

This facilitated the challenge of the rationalists to reduce history to nonsense.

Yet a cautious examination of information famous that the fact is an entire lot more complex, charming and disconcerting.

Above all, people who witnessed the events Enfield haven't any doubt to were involved in a actual case of obsession, and however the fact that their memories may also moreover appear exaggerated, it's also not possible that so character witnesses also can were abused.

Key impartial witnesses, there were law enforcement officials who have been referred to as to the home of Hodgson fast after the poltergeist has made its presence felt for the number one time in August 1977.

They took the evidence and located the real terror of the family however within the absence of concrete evidence, they were skeptical approximately what can also want to have occurred.

Only whilst the officers had been primed from which they had been compelled to take the case more seriously:

pretty , a living room chair has raised the carpet inside the the front of their eyes and started to move slowly inside the direction of the room.

"He has raised about 1 cm" remembers Carolyn Heeps, a Metropolitan Police officers sent to research the haunting.

"I observed him slide to the right on a bit over 1 m in advance than stopping.

I checked to peer if he ought to have slipped by myself. I even positioned a ball on the ground to peer if it might roll in the same route because the chair.

She did not do it.

I checked if there were no son under the cushions and chairs and I actually have not seen. I couldn't discover any rationalization. "

But of course, no crime were devoted whilst the police could not assist extra.

Desperate to discover an cause of what modified into taking location of their home, the own family grew to end up to the Society for Psychical Research, a reputable clinical body analyzing instances of alleged hauntings from a theoretical perspective.

They sent investigators, Guy Lyon Playfair and Maurice Grosse, to study the proof.

And to save you any claim of fraud, the corporation added in an independent prison professional, Mary Rose Barrington, recheck for all their artwork.

This became to make certain that there can be no credible claim that the two researchers were in any other case as meticulous, sincere and unbiased in their investigations.

Obviously, over the subsequent 14 months they spent at the case, the two researchers have compiled pretty a few inexplicable phenomena.

Boxes had been flying thru the rooms, trinkets floated in the air, books regarded and disappeared mysteriously.

pix have to pay attention noises inside the walls.

It become actually bizarre however worse turn out to be to return again.

One morning, on the equal time as Guy Playfair turned into on foot inside the house, he heard a "Huge vibration noise."

"I in fact concept someone pierced a large hole inside the wall of the residence," he said.

"I rushed into the room and there was a huge bang. The whole chimney became torn. It have end up the type of vintage Victorian forged iron stoves which must have weighed at least 30 kg.

It turn out to be so heavy that I couldn't even increase it. The youngsters might not need to rip the wall.

It come to be really not possible. We recorded the incident on tape, collectively with the chimney being torn off the wall.

The sports activities might speedy take a more disturbing turn. Late one nighttime, whilst the children have been dozing in their room and Maurice Grosse referred to the results of the day, he have become via Janet cry.

Maurice ran to the bottom of the stairs to appearance the 12 one year antique girl reputedly be drawn from his room by using using an invisible pressure. Janet become dragged down the stairs and fell to the toes of Maurice.

Janet and Margaret ejected from their beds

This incident have emerge as moreover recorded on tape and became the primary of several incidents in which the poltergeist took Janet and searching for to win.

Shortly after, we even located Janet go with the waft in the air and this time there had been unbiased witnesses.

A settlement and a baker who handed every have taken a have a look at the residence and discovered Janet reputedly levitating above the mattress thru a top floor window.

As Janet recollects:

"The girl noticed me turn and hit in opposition to the window.

I idea I grow to be going to interrupt the window and get thru. Many children fantasize approximately flying but it changed into now not like that.

When you levitate strain and you do no longer comprehend if you may land, it is very scary.

I nevertheless do no longer understand the way it came about. "

And that come to be now not all. Apparently prey to three tough power, Janet began to swear and scream insults at individuals who had been inside the room of a disembodied voice that did not sound like his.

So changed into it proof of a poltergeist or virtually a little one who changed into a farce ?

Investigators began to impeach

"Spirit" and the solutions they obtained had been decidedly sinister. The poltergeist recognized himself to a person named Bill who defined "have had a hemorrhage, sleeping and having useless in a chair within the corner down the steps."

What could this suggest ?

Surprisingly, next research has confirmed that prolonged in advance than Hodgson will pass into the residence, an vintage man named Bill Wilkins had certainly lived there.

He died of a cerebral hemorrhage sitting in a chair.

This is without a doubt an exciting tale.

But is it honestly a established case of poltergeist?

If you dig underneath the floor, doubts quick start to emerge.

On numerous sports activities, the ladies on the center of the case were taken into playing guidelines investigators.

Once, they have been taken to cover the Guy recorder.

They had bear in mind to argue that the poltergeist had prevailed.

Unfortunately for the women, turning the recorder and recorded their shot.

"They were no longer exceptional for gambling pranks" Guy recollects.

"We constantly caught them. What do you count on from children? I might be greater worried in the occasion that that that they had no longer entertained every so often.

I mean, they behaved like regular youngsters. "

Asked approximately these jokes these days, Janet says she and her sister have simply made jokes due to the fact they were uninterested in being tested all the time.

They had grow to be like animals in a zoo who are continuously asked to do hints for definitely happy spectators.

People predicted that some issue inexplicable takes location, and whilst no longer some thing befell, the women decided to make a funny story at the time.

But, and that is critical, Janet estimates that only 1 to two% hundreds of numerous paranormal phenomena that happened within the residence had been his and Margaret made and it modified into minor things like a chair to face on above a door and fake it modified right into a poltergeist who had.

In addition, in plenty of times, it would had been physical not viable for the ladies to have faked the proof.

How can a 12 year vintage preserve close a fire or levitate a chair inside the the front of cops ?

Chapter 6: Levitated Item In The Chamber
Janet And Margaret

America

The Bell Witch 1817

 John Bell House

John Bell, a farmer from North Carolina, changed into installation north of Robertson County Tennessee in 1804.

His land of 320 acres of specific farming land ranged along the Red River. They had a non violent lifestyles inside the course of the first 13 years of their lifestyles there.

He and his own family had been individuals of the Baptist Church of Red River and John became the pastor. The circle of relatives has grown and has end up rich.

At the prevent of the summer season of 1817 something befell that changed their lives for all time.

Some circle of relatives participants commenced out to appearance amazing animals across the assets.

Then, past due at night time, they heard knocking on doors and outdoors walls of the house.

Then it is in the house they heard them.

It turned into the noise of chains dragged along the floors of the residence, the sounds of a rat gnawing the posts beds, stones fell on the timber floors and the noise of someone who is choking.

The circle of relatives changed into terrified but they stored the decision of the game trouble for at least one year.

Later, subjects have end up intolerable whilst John confided to a neighbor, James Johnson.

He invited Mr. Johnson and his wife to spend the night time with him.

After a few nights in the house, Mr. Johnson advocated Bell to speak to one in every of a type human beings.

They then common a committee and an research is in followed.

It have become no longer very prolonged earlier than people for kilometers round come to see with their personal eyes the sports that terrorized the Bell own family.

By now, this evil strain had amplified a lot that she now had a voice.

When requested this invisible strain that she emerge as, she gave one of a kind identities.

It have grow to be hooked up with the aid of using a neighbor that he definitely emerge as a lady who became suspected of being a witch named Kate Batts.

That's what each person started out to accept as authentic with and that is why we known as the invisible pressure Kate Bell Witch.

It seemed that Kate had critical motives for travelling the house of Bell.

The first changed into to kill John Bell.

Why?

Nobody knows, Kate never intended reason.

The 2d motive have turn out to be to save you the younger John Bell, Betsy, to marry a neighbor known as Joshua Gardner.

During the following three years, Kate has plagued the circle of relatives individuals nearly each day.

John and his daughter Betsy had been people who acquired the worst physical abuse.

Betsy have come to be hair pulling, pinching, scratching with a pin or even overwhelmed through way of the invisible stress.

John for his detail had throat which swelled and he had a sense someone sticking a stick in the mouth.

Then he started out to lose manipulate of his facial muscle agencies.

With time, he have become an increasing number of susceptible.

Kate have grow to be famous and attracted growing crowds.

She regarded very informed on many topics; the Bible, and the beyond and destiny of the human beings.

She want to, it became said, be in two locations on the equal time to kilometers.

Kate finally completed his challenge at the farm Bell.

December 20, 1820, John Bell died.

Tomb of John Bell

He may additionally moreover were poisoned thru way of Kate and she or he took all the credit score score for what they are pronouncing.

Then in March 1821 the younger Betsy broke off her engagement to Joshua Gardner.

Kate then stated good-bye to every body and promised to head back in seven years.

She another time in 1828 for some weeks.

During her visit she can also want to have come chat with John Bell Jr. And had long conversations with him about the beyond and destiny. She ought to have made some predictions.

She additionally instructed him that there was a motive the torments his father however in no manner decided wherein.

After this go to she informed him that she would move returned in 107 years.

Which leads us in 1935.

But many consider that she has in no way left the region due to the many activities that have came about close by.

There are severa books on the priority and the legend of the Bell Witch is a part of the Tennessee history.

There are organized companies travelling the lands of Bell mainly at some degree within the Halloween length.

One can also additionally even lease a deliver and go to the cave of the witch at some point of certain periods of the year.

cave of the witch

Haunting Sisters Fox

1848

Kate, Margaretta and Leah Fox

It is a phenomenon of fear that drew hobby to the manifestations of spirits in America within the 19th century.

Blows, which no person can also want to bet the purpose, were heard for the number one time in 1846 in a known as Veckmann, dwelling within the house of a small village called Hydesville inside the country of New York.

Nothing changed into left out to discover the author of those mysterious sounds, but we're able to benefit.

Six months later, in 1847, the circle of relatives left the residence which changed into then inhabited via a member of the Methodist Episcopal Church:

Mr. John Fox and his circle of relatives, which includes his partner and daughters, Margaret then aged 14 and Kate, 11 years. The Fox own family consisted of six kids but handiest Margaret and Kate have been residing with their parents.

For 3 months they were quiet there, then commenced out out over again blows extra difficult.

At first they have been very moderate noises as although a person knocked at the floor of one of the bedrooms, and on every occasion, a vibration changed into felt on the floor; is the equal perceived lying.

The floor have end up vibrating so difficult that the shaking beds and we felt this vibration at the same time as reputation on the floor.

domestic of the Fox sisters

The images had been heard with out preventing, there has been no way to sleep inside the house.

March 31, 1848, Mrs. Fox and her daughters, now not able to sleep for the night time, and pressured thru fatigue, went to mattress early, in the identical room, hoping to break out the sports activities which typically produced in the middle of night.

Mr. Fox have end up away.

Soon beatings commenced once more, and the 2 girls, wakened through the noise, start to imitate the snapping their arms.

To their astonishment blows answered each slam, then the youngest Miss Kate women desired to affirm this surprising; she made a snap, they heard a shot, , 3, and so on., and however be invisible agent or lower back the same amount of strokes. His sister stated jokingly:

" Now do as I depend one, , three, four, and so on. ... "

hitting every in his hand the range indicated.

The blows observed with the equal precision, but this sign of intelligence alarming the lady, she rapid ceased revel in.

Mrs. Fox said,

 "In ten".

The officer struck ten times.

The mom asked a series of questions and the solutions given by using way of figures confirmed extra understanding of its very non-public affairs than she had herself; due to the fact the blows insisted she had seven children at the same time as she modified into protesting no longer having given shipping to six till a seventh died early, came decrease back to him.

To this question :

"Are you a person, you hit that? "

no answer came; however it

 "Are you a spirit ? "

became spoke back with the useful resource of sharp, quick strokes. They known as a neighbor, Mrs. Redfield his enjoyment grew to turn out to be to amazement after which in terror As she listened, too, the proper solutions to intimate questions.

Mrs. Fox stated to his invisible interlocutor:

" If we did come the friends, they hold to fulfill the blows? "

A shot changed into heard in sign of affirmation.

The pals called no longer lengthy coming, counting discover the invisible hitter via all feasible surveillance; but the accuracy of some of information given and stroke, in reaction to questions addressed to the invisible, on particular instances of every, glad the most incredulous.

The sound of these items unfold a protracted way and large, and soon arrived from all sides of priests, judges, scientific medical medical doctors, and a crowd of residents.

Neighbors flocked at the equal time as rumors were spreading about this marvel; the 2 children have been taken thru one in every of them on the equal time as Mrs. Fox become going to spend the night time time at Mrs. Redfield.

In their absence, the phenomenon endured exactly as in advance than, which as soon as and for all to silence all the ones toe crunching theories and dislocated knees perfectly blind to the facts so regularly advanced.

All manner of monitoring have been completed to discover the invisible hitter, but the research of the family, and the entire network, grow to be unnecessary.

They could not find out a herbal motive these singular activities.

The experiments observed, severa and precise.

The following Sunday, the house have become packed, extra than 3 hundred people have been gift at that issue.

The curious, attracted with the resource of way of these new phenomena, now not content material cloth more requests and responses.

One of them, named Isaac Post, had the concept to recite aloud the letters of the alphabet, asking the Spirit to kindly hit a blow to folks that composed the terms he desired to recognize .

From that day, the non secular telegraphy changed into located:

This technique is one that we are capable of observe the turntables.

Sisters Fox-spiritualist seance

This became the primary conversation that befell in present day instances and that we've got were given found, some of the beings of the alternative international and this one.

In this manner, Ms. Fox got here to understand that the spirit answered, have come to be that of someone who've been murdered in the house she lived severa years ago, he became named Charles B. Rosma, that it turned into a peddler and thirty-one, at the same time as the person with whom he become staying killed him for his cash and buried within the cellar.

Human bones had been genuinely found later.

That, in all its simplicity, the begin of the phenomenon that might revolutionize the area.

Denied thru the professional scholars, mocked with the aid of the press of every worlds, blacklisted by the usage of the usage of stressful and jealous religions suspect to justice, exploited thru manner of shameless charlatans, Spiritualism come to be, however, make its manner and overcome adherents, the decide rises to numerous million, as it has the maximum effective pressure than some thing else:

The truth.

The Spirit advocated the women to public conferences wherein he may additionally want to convince skeptics of its existence.

The Fox circle of relatives went to settle in Rochester and, following the recommendation of their buddy from location, those more youthful missionaries did now not hesitate to brave the Protestant fanaticism via offering to publish to greater stringent manipulate.

Accused of fraud and ordered the ministers of their religion to barren location the ones practices, Mr. And Mrs. Fox is creating a remarkable responsibility to unfold the knowledge of those phenomena, which they considered a incredible and consoling truth useful for all , refused to place up and have been pushed out of their church.

The fanatics who collected around them had been struck with the identical disapproval.

The fanatical conservatives brought the populace in the direction of the Fox own family.

The apostles of the contemporary faith then supplied to the overall public proof of the truth of events earlier than the overall public assembly in Corynthial Hall, the most important room within the town.

They started out with a conference in which the development of the phenomenon have been exposed for the purpose that early days.

This conversation, greeted with boos, but ends in the appointment of a rate to take a look at the information; towards the general expectation, and in opposition to his personal conviction, the fee emerge as forced to admit that once the maximum careful interest, she must discover no trace of fraud.

They brought that the ones pix got here on partitions and doors a protracted manner women, inflicting high-quality vibration. They completely did not find out any approach by means of which one may also need to get.

We immediately appointed a 2nd committee that resorted to even extra rigorous investigative techniques; they made are searching for or even undress mediums, with the useful resource of manner of ladies of course, we continually heard rappings (raps in the desk), transferring furnishings, solutions to all questions, even intellectual; no ventriloquism, no subterfuge, no question.

Second document more favorable than the primary, in great suitable religion spiritualists and the fact of the excellent phenomenon.

It isn't feasible - says Ms. Hardinge - to describe the indignation that became manifested in this second disappointment.

The very last record said that the noises were heard and that their complete examination confirmed decisively that they had been produced by the use of both a mechanism nor ventriloquism, despite the fact that, about the character of the agent that produced them, they were no longer able to determine.

A 1/3 committee end up straight away decided on some of the unbelievers and scoffers extra.

The cease result of those investigations, even more outrageous than the opportunity for bad women, grew to end up extra than ever to the confusion of their detractors.

The committee then testified that their questions, a few posed mentally, had acquired accurate solutions.

The crowd, enraged, satisfied of the treachery of the Commissioners and their connivance with impostors, stated that if the report end up favorable, it lynch mediums and their attorneys.

The ladies, but their terror, escorted with the resource of way of circle of relatives and a few buddies, do no longer provided inside the assembly and took the extent of the hall, all determined to die, if critical, Martyrs an unpopular but indeniable fact.

 The record was made by the usage of a member of the price who had vowed to find out the trick, however he needed to admit that the purpose of knocks, regardless of the maximum careful research, it become unknown.

Immediately took place a frightful tumult:

The mob desired to lynch the ladies, and they were without the intervention of a Quaker named George Villets, which made them a rampart of his frame and brought the employer to greater human emotions.

We see from this story that Spiritualism changed into critically studied from the start.

These aren't fine pals, more or a amazing deal tons much less ignorant, who see an inexplicable, however the committees, often appointed, which, after thorough investigations, are obliged to apprehend certainly the authenticity of the phenomenon.

Attempts to find out fraud within the phenomena befell regularly.

Note that this event, that's the delivery of spiritualism, is situation to many distortions and misinformation at the a part of opponents of spiritualism.

Thus the Jesuit Lucien Roure, in his ebook "The excellent spiritualist"Claims that no one had requested whether the phenomenon emerge as due to the deception and leaves even insinuate that they have been produced thru the play of the toe or ankle.

Others pass so far that the youngest daughter was a ventriloquist.

These assertions, unsubstantiated, can deliver an reason for the consequences of discovered phenomena, and affirmed their authenticity through destructive and fanatical fee.

Chapter 7: The Turntables

The tale of the Fox sisters unfold speedy, and anywhere have been held demonstrations via what modified into then called the religious telegraphy.

It quickly grew bored with so inconvenient device, and hitters indiquèrent themselves a new mode of conversation.

You in truth needed to meet round a table, place arms over, and lifted the desk ought to strike a blow, on the identical time as you recite the alphabet on every of the letters that the spirit may supply.

This manner, regardless of the fact that very gradual, produced brilliant outcomes, and we were given his rotating and speaking tables.

It have to be said that the table became now not restrained to face on one foot to answer questions located to him, she waved in all guidelines, turning underneath the hands of the experimenters, occasionally rose into the air without that one also can want to peer the maintaining strain for that reason suspended.

Other instances the answers were made using small strokes, grow to be heard within the interior of the wooden.

These everyday records attracted current day hobby and shortly fashion turntables invades the whole of America.

The table taught over again a more speedy method.

On his instructions, we tailored to a triangular board with wheels 3 feet, and one in every of them, they mounted a pencil, then positioned the device on a sheet of paper, and the medium laid fingers on the middle of this small desk.

We then noticed the pencil tracing letters, then sentences, and shortly the board wrote rapid and gave messages. Later despite the fact that, it have become determined that the board come to be certainly unnecessary, and that it modified into enough to really positioned his midrange armed with a pencil on paper, and that the spirit have become the act mechanically.

Besides the moderate those who spent their time questioning minds on their issues of affection life, or a misplaced object, intense minds, scientists, thinkers, attracted with the resource of using the noise that grow to be made round the ones phenomena, resolved examine scientifically, to location their human beings on protect toward what they called a contagious madness.

In 1856, Judge Edmonds, juris are in search of advice from eminent who enjoys unquestioned authority in the New World, posted a ebook on research he had undertaken with the idea of demonstrating the falsity of spiritual phenomena; the give up give up result have come to be diametrically detrimental and Edmond choose out recounted the truth of these outstanding activities.

The Mapes trainer who taught chemistry at the National Academy of the usa, gave himself as an awful lot as a rigorous studies that consequences because of the reality the previous one, in a reasoned announcement, consistent with which the phenomena were properly because of the intervention of spirits .

But what produced the greatest impact, it changed into converted to the new mind of the famous Robert Hare, a professor at the University of Pennsylvania, which scientifically experimented motion tables and recorded his research in 1856 in a amount entitled

Experimental investigations of the spirit manifestation

 Therefore, the warfare amongst skeptics and believers engaged certainly.

Writers, students, audio device, clergymen, threw themselves into the fray, and to offer an idea of development taken with the aid of the communicate, it suffices to bear in thoughts that already in 1854 signed a petition of 15,000 names residents, turn out to be presented at the Congress headquarters in Washington to invite him to rent a price to examine current spiritualism (it's the name we provide to America in spiritualism).

This request became rejected by means of the assembly, but the momentum become given and that they saw stand up companies that primarily based newspapers in which persisted the conflict in competition to unbelievers.

In 1852, the first Congress Spiritualist (the phrase modified into not invented however) took place in Cleveland.

American spiritualists sent after the Congress of mediums in vintage Europe.

tables It twirled in France in 1853. It turn out to be stated in all schooling of society that this new; one every so often addressed without the sacramental question:

" Well ! Do you switch the tables? "Then, as all that is fashion, after a 2d of fashion, tables ceased to occupy the eye, which fell on distinct objects.

This mania to reveal the tables in spite of the fact that had an vital result, it become to make people assume severa people approximately the possibility of the relationship among dwelling and lifeless.

In 1854 we then had greater than 3 million fans in America and tens of hundreds of mediums.

The fanatics moreover have become severa in France, but though lacked a actual clarification, theoretical and sensible, of the uncommon phenomenon.

That's on the equal time as Allan Kardec who cared for thirty years the so-known as phenomena of animal magnetism, hypnotism and somnambulism, and who observed within the new phenomenon that a fairy tale , attended several classes spiritualists a good way to scrutinize the validity of these appearances.

Far from being an enthusiast of these sports, and absorbed through his one of a kind obligations, he have become approximately to give up while family gave him fifty one of a type communique specs received five years and asked him to summarize:

Thus was born the Book of Spirits.

 Poltergeist Miami

1966/1967

A very precise haunting, very active, came about in January 1967 and lasted a touch more than 1 one year, mysteriously beginning and finishing like most poltergeist times, Tropication Arts, a Miami enterprise that sells and painted souvenirs.

It could in all likelihood emerge as one of the maximum exciting cases and super documented of poltergeist form of anxiety within the United States, attended via manner of the use of employees, pals, personnel, officials, preachers, media, a magician, investigators paranormal and para-psychologists famend.

The interest consisted of a smart go with the flow and breaking devices within the corporation organisation warehouse.

It from time to time passed off to a most of 15 witnesses at a time.

The worry has been surely documented via the usage of manner of the writer and investigator of ghosts, Susy Smith, who arrived on the scene at the begin that weird hobby come to be growing.

Susy arrived early and left as past due as feasible, searching at and taking unique notes in the course of 24 days.

300 man or woman incidents passed off all through his stay.

She has accumulated memories of scientists, reporters, magicians and lots of others in the path of his studies.

The specialists in the above regions additionally scrutinized the business, outside and inside, for any evidence of trickery or fraud.

No top notch forestall may be approximately the poltergeist that moved some of the human beings and investigators, except that it become actually paranormal, some issue uncommon to study first appearance.

HOW THE PHENOMENON A POLTERGEIST THERE BEGINS:

Most witnesses are first to exclaim Susy

"I do not count on so, but that is in truth the case. "

Ruth May, who labored there delivered:

"I do now not believe in ghosts ... But a few factor we can't see, looking for to make the mess in our warehouse. "

About a month earlier than the interest will become heavy, Ruth instructed Susy a cup of occasional beer harm and she or he definitely concept that some of the male humans have been gambling video games inside the over again room.

It ordered them to be extra careful however they insisted that they'd no longer damaged glassware.

The proprietors did no longer receive as actual with them to start with; But rapid, they may revel in all topics crashing on the same time as additionally at the back inside the warehouse.

FALLING OBJECTS DURING HUNTING:

It come to be not unusual for the ghost, or something, to push one or boxes of the enterprise's shelf.

He may pick to hit an man or woman object. The frequency of fallen and beaten gadgets have end up alarming to observers, even though, as he need to supply a fall after some different in collection moreover.

Note, this poltergeist would possibly wreck or may additionally drop subjects on request in a few unspecified time within the destiny of some exams which have been run.

For example, a Coca Cola bottle have come to be positioned on a shelf wherein no individual have to get proper of entry to it with out being determined.

The research organization located the location in which the bottle changed into placed till they are distracted, but most effective for a 2nd, for some issue else taking place within the warehouse.

Then, the bottle fell and grow to be damaged to quantities.

No one have become near her or could have been the dropping of wherein it end up located.

Any dish or dishes that changed into positioned there for the invisible pressure breakage during next trials brought about a comparable cease end result.

The poltergeist broke topics voluntarily. But only if the vicinity had not been knowingly monitored for disruption.An object, a pitcher, became visible falling to the floor through the use of a person and a lady; But how they fell changed into strange.

The glass bounced and shook a chunk at the start, then he fell to the ground at an perspective, as though a stress had dropped gravely.

Another man who changed into moreover witness stated he grow to be raised inside the air first, then flew right all the manner down to the ground.

ATTEMPTED THE DEBUG POLTERGEIST:

A magician, Howard Brooks, have end up tremendous a person have become deceiving every body, then he started out to find out who and the way.

Brooks emerge as first instructed the proprietor:

"What form of idiot do you, obviously you've got have been given an employee who plays tricks.

I can do topics myself crashing shelves, too, whilst no person is close to me ... Any magician can. "

The expert of magic after looking and investigating accidents due to the poltergeist to say:

The warehouse modified into 30 x 50 ft and had shelves that stretched over 4 lanes.

It changed into critical to understand because of the reality the poltergeist regularly broke some issue in a single driveway, drawing the attention of all people.

And while this alley became watched closely, a few element else might be damaged in a few other aisle as though the primary fairway modified proper right into a distraction, and so forth.

After loads research and studies, Brooks must haven't any success in finding this magic as it become not a trick.

The para-psychologist noted WG Roll, the Psychical Research Foundation in Durham, North Carolina, investigated the case with Dr. J. Gaither Pratt Duke University and the University of Virginia.

WG Roll grow to be quoted saying:

"I even have decided no proof that the phenomena have been due to normal method."

Dr. Pratt summarizes the obsession with:

"I do not forget the case well worth of careful check and reviews within the medical literature of parapsychology."

YOUNG MAN IN WAREHOUSE FLORIDA ....

THEORY ON POLTERGEIST FLORIDA:

In most poltergeist instances, someone is usually observed to be the middle, the center of the phenomenon, unexplained, or great interest.

Some say that "Poltergeists draw close-out human beings rather than homes."

Therefore, it changed into believed that psychokinetic stress the important figure unconsciously produced paranormal events.

In almost all times studied, the number one decide is a female.

In this unusual case, a more youthful man who worked on the warehouse have become in the long run theorized because the center of the conduct.

Perhaps frustration that he may also need to appear through accident as paranormal hobby inside the warehouse?

Investigators had been satisfied that he have turn out to be the middle of the haunting.

And after some of attempting out, the younger man appeared to have the abilties of psychokinesis - "the spirit of the consequences of the material."The haunting ceased after the person had left the corporation.

Julio then labored with different organizations, and become decided with the beneficial useful resource of the identical poltergeist hobby.

Belgium

the phenomena ofBow-Wattripont 1993

January 1993 activities unfold within the small metropolis of Arc-Wattripont near Tournai in Belgium in a residence inhabited via an aged couple, the father is a truck riding pressure.

Besides the 2 proprietors, of their son and their daughter lodged there, and Eric, the latter boyfriend.

Unemployed and private domestic due to own family problems, there was hosted due to the truth thirteen December 1992.

The host own family can be very religious, bordering bigotry.

From the number one days of 1993, unexplained incidents.

They attain an unsustainable level inside the midnight of five January, leading the owner to name the police at 22 h 30.

The first patrol were given there can be shocked to discover the family man carrying a tough hat for protection from projectiles.

At first incredulous, the police find themselves the strangeness of events, main them to request each one of a kind patrol coming in to help verify the information and take part in studies.

Two nights, the police witness journey and falling gadgets, the desk at which sat a policeman moving from fifteen centimeters while it's miles the splendid nearby.

A milk discipline is screened on the ceiling and falls with an now not probable direction.

A footboard is smashed via using manner of a huge hole that is prolonged in advance than witnesses.

the bed bed down in which Eric is lying lifts thirty cm for numerous seconds.

The scene is filmed by means of body of workers camcorder from a policeman, but the pix are of horrible extraordinary.

Over a dozen policemen of diverse ranks and police commissioner whose witness of the data.

The painstaking excavations that were without delay agencies do no longer work.

According to preliminary findings, evidently the younger Eric is at the epicenter of the protests.

Following an exorcism performed by a clergyman of the Gallican Church and the remoteness of the younger man in every other housing troubles cease.

The public prosecutor of Tournai opened an investigation and one in all his first choices is to limit members of the safety forces and communicate at the concern.

The video tape recorded through the police is positioned below seal.

The indisputable purpose factors are inaccessible, numerous fake and unfounded rumors circulate such intervention Gérard Majax or Bogdanov brothers.

It follows endless controversies about the individual of the records that have been exaggerated or maybe their very fact, some media - collectively with TV channel - up to complete, specialists and witnesses in assist, "that he had in truth nothing uncommon occurred on this residence, if no longer the moves of a loopy candy ".

In 1999 Yves Lignon advised in taken into consideration simply one among his books of tales from 21 to 22 January with the aid of a physics professor from a police officer and of his deputies who participated inside the studies.

These verify the various activities they attended, which includes the episode of the milk jug and the hole inside the footboard

From 2010, an intensive studies is achieved with the useful resource of the CERPI, a Belgian enterprise for studies on unexplained phenomena which, after checking the principle elements of the case and gathered the direct memories of numerous policemen who experienced those sports activities, posted in 2015 his conclusions usually tend to demonstrate, with supporting evidence, that incomprehensible records have actually passed off within the path of nights.

footboard is smashed with the resource of a massive hollow and cupboard reversed

 Canada

the thriller of Amerst 1878-1879

Chapter 8: One Of The Maximum Terrifying Paranormal Facts

Esther Cox of Amherst

For months, an entity has plagued a female of nineteen years and his family with loud noises, horrible threats and unspeakable violence and feature come to be in one of the most well-known poltergeist case of Canada and one of the maximum effective within the international.

The case of Esther Cox of Amherst, who have grow to be the victim in a case that has become a poltergeist memories scariest of Canadian statistics.

The peculiar occasions had been located and documented with the resource of many humans, or actually have become the priority of a e-book.

We are in 1878 in Princess Street in Amherst, a town in north-applicable Nova Scotia, the New Brunswick border to Canada.

Esther Cox, 19, was dwelling in a "small" residence rented alongside along with his married sister Olive Teed, her husband Daniel Teed and their younger kids.

The small crowded cabin additionally housed siblings Esther Jennie and William and Daniel's brother, John.

House of Esther Cox

Suddenly, inside the tedium of this everyday home, horror struck.

But no pressure paranormal, as an alternative a human monster:

Esther have become nearly raped by manner of an acquaintance named Bob MacNeal, a cobbler whose Esther knew recognition as an alternative dangerous ...

Although she escaped her rapist with minor accidents, violence in opposition to him, has apparently it opened a door for specific attacks,

this time from one or extra invisible entities .
The poltergeist mystery commenced out
Amherst.

Although the residence became entire of Teed
and their own family, it changed into now not
unusual for owners take residents to pay lease.

Walter Hubbell, an actor at the time, become a
boarder on the residence in which Teed whilst
the primary tremors of supernatural
phenomena occurred modified into, and he
even described them in this e-book, The Great
Amherst Mystery.

One night time, cries of worry leads all tenants
of the house to hurry into the room wherein
Esther and Jennie sisters percent a bed

The women found some element forming
below their blankets even as they had been
making geared up to sleep for the night time
time time; Esther notion it became a mouse.

But a are searching for did no longer art work.
The girls went lower back to mattress and the
house modified into quiet for the night time
time.

The subsequent night time time, greater screams disturbed the family.

Esther and Jennie excitedly allege they heard unusual noises coming from a trunk of antique tissue that was stored beneath their mattress

When they brought the sector to the middle of the room, she "jumped" into the air itself and landed on its factor.

Immediately, the ladies nervously repositioned the field at the same time as she yet again jumped into the air, inflicting the more youthful girls screaming.

Until now, the sports activities might be attributed to the active creativeness of the ladies, in particular if we remember cutting-edge-day and painful experience of Esther inside the fingers of Bob MacNeal.

However, the zero.33 night time after the first event, everybody felt that a few element changed into wrong with Esther Cox.

That night time time, Esther apologized to visit mattress early complaining of being feverish.

Around 22 pm, rapid after Jennie is joined in mattress, Esther jumped from the bed to the middle of the room, tearing her night time garments and shouting:

"My God! What is taking area to me? I die!"

Jennie lit a lamp and checked out her sister, horrified to appearance that her skin was great purple and seemed to swell abnormally.

Olive, her sister rushed into the room to help Jennie to deliver their sister in bed, as she seemed to choke and function trouble respiration.

The particular adults watched in disbelief the whole body of Esther, remarkably heat to the touch, swollen and reddened.

Esther's eyes swelled and moreover crying in ache, afraid of literally burst into the room via his pores and pores and skin increasingly stretched.

Then, below Esther's mattress, a deaf and deafening noise - like a thunderbolt - shook the room. Three exceptional noises exploded underneath the bed, then swelling of Esther disappeared after which fall right into a deep sleep.

Four nights later, the ones terrifying sports activities are repeated, unexplained swelling and torture Esther terminate only through the stormy noises below the bed

Unable to cope with this unlucky ordeal, Daniel requested a local physician, Dr. Carritte, have a examine Esther.

Esther attended the bedside, he watched with astonishment flow into his pillow underneath his head, at the same time as the fingers of the woman have been hooked up the front of him.

He heard loud banging under the bed, but watching it determined no motive to offer an motive of it. Then he observed the bedclothes thrown sooner or later of the room with the resource of invisible fingers.

The medical physician then heard a scratching noise, like a steel tool scratching the plaster.

The Doctor looked at the wall above Esther's mattress and observed letters from extra than 30 cm excessive which have been engraved on the wall.

When the textual content have end up subsequently examine, it come to be written in words.

ESTHER COX YOU ARE MINE TO KILL

that could bring about:

ESTHER COX YOU ARE TO ME TO KILL

Then a pile of shredded plaster came off the wall, crossed the room and landed the physician's toes.

After hours, the house is again silent.

Dr. Carritte with the aid of braveness or compassion interest decrease back the next day and testified greater unexplained sports.

Potatoes within the kitchen threw themselves in the course of rooms and deafening noises now regarded to return from the roof of the house, the medical doctor himself examined the roof and there has been no obvious reason.

These sports and years later, he wrote to a fellow medical medical doctor:

"People have been skeptical certainly in all situations fast satisfied that n 'there has been no fraud or deception inside the case. If I posted the case in medical journals, as you recommend, I doubt it's miles believed by means of manner of manner of doctors in famous. I'm positive I might not have notion of such subjects if I had no longer witnessed. "

Obviously, the medical doctor could not carry out a touch problem to assist Esther or settle troubles house Teed.

The obsession continued and, in fact, have come to be an increasing number of adverse and menacing:

•Unexplained fires broke out throughout the residence.

•Knives and forks were thrown violently to paste in wood.

•Matches lit materialized amid rooms for fallen at the beds.

•Furniture moved themselves, reversing himself or slammed in opposition to the partitions.

•They heard the loud slapping sound, followed via the usage of manner of the advent of purple finger marks at the face of Esther.

•sewing pins have seemed from nowhere and had been projected in the face of Esther.

•A knife was ripped from the hand of a boy inside the network to locate himself inside the again of Esther.

•And many more (flying chair, table lifts

Poor and tormented, Esther tried numerous instances to interrupt out the evil entity, however she determined her anywhere she went.

One Sunday, Esther attended a baptism and sat in one of the benches in the room.

Once started baptism, knocks and "Reminders" echoed at some degree in the church, seeming to go back decrease lower back from the the front.

The sounds have grow to be stronger and stronger, drowning out the speech of the priest.

Knowing that she come to be the cause, Esther left the constructing and the noises are robotically stopped.

She additionally tried to save his family from the evil torment she suffered.

At first, she moved into the house of a neighbor, however the poltergeist positioned, compelled to go domestic.

Owner Teed, fearing the unfavorable nature of the phenomenon, favored to evict the circle of relatives.

Again, taking obligation for the occasions, Esther moved and determined art work at a close-by farm.

However, even as the barn of the farm mysteriously burned, the farmer Esther arrested for arson and turned into sentenced to 4 months in prison.

Fortunately, Esther has served one month in prison and have become launched.

The short imprisonment segment can also moreover moreover first regarded to be a terrible detail for Esther, but it had its extremely good issue.

After she has truely been released from prison, poltergeist hobby appears clearly begin to fade.

There have been minor incidents in a short time period, but the obsession eventually forestall absolutely.

Esther changed into later married instances, and died in 1912 at the age of fifty 3 years.

After his dying, the ebook The Great Amherst Mystery is out.

It included testimony from sixteen witnesses signed the terrible sports lived in Amherst.

Ontario

Poltergeist St. Catharines 1970

According to Bob Crawford, close by police officer retired Niagara whilst he answered to a domestic dispute at 237 Church Street, condominium 1, St. Catharines (Ontario), the "Garden City" of Canada, February 6, 1970, the spirit was a poltergeist.

The poltergeist was raised via the use of way of the media in the Niagara Peninsula, as well as via manner of national and international media, which includes CBC, CTV, CHML, The St. Catharines Standard, The Canadian Press, The Hamilton Spectator, The Toronto Telegram, Toronto Daily News, and the Buffalo Evening News, to call some.

Monday 2 October 1995, at a domestic in St. Catharines, I interviewed Bob Crawford, Bill and Mike Weir McMenanin, all retired participants of the Regional Police Force stationed in St. Niagara Catharines.

Mr. Crawford recalled how, on 6 February 1970 as he left the 237 Church Street, rental 1, in which he had been sent to research a domestic dispute, a girl who come to be recognized as a resident of a few distinctive constructing the condominium requested the officer his assist in their apartment.

Crawford followed the citizen in their apartment come to be in disarray.

The complainant knowledgeable the agent his tale of strategies items and furnishings moved round their apartment with the useful resource of manner of unseen forces.

Crawford showed a cloth cabinet mendacity on her facet within the kitchen.

Crawford was knowledgeable that the items and furnishings started out out to move themselves of their small apartment to the road from the church approximately 10 days in advance than February 6, 1970.

After being attentive to the complainant and the activities surrounding the modern-day-day u . S . Of the condominium, Crawford claimed that his first notion became to name a priest, while a priest of a community Roman Catholic church got here to the condo.

Crawford said the priest grow to be properly privy to the activities unfolding within the Church Street apartment and there has been visible a mattress faraway from a wall thru itself.

The priest pushed the mattress to the wall, however even as he grew to grow to be his head, the mattress a long way from the wall with the aid of the use of unseen forces.

Crawford asked that everyone tries to live calm and requested them to go into the living room.

Since Crawford turned into the very last man or woman to go away the kitchen, he claimed to have moved a chair out of his way and located the chair in a regular function in the direction of the kitchen desk earlier than getting into the residing room.

While in search of to calm the complainant, Crawford and the priest head to the sound of stepping into the living room and the kitchen.

Crawford stated that he and the priest had entered the kitchen and declared that the chair he had moved closer to the kitchen desk become within the middle of the kitchen some meters from the kitchen desk.

The priest knowledgeable Crawford which have emerge as the form of event that befell considering 10 days.

It is about this time that Weir gendarmes arrived.

Bill Weir policeman who believed Crawford assist at a country wide call, come to be about to make a "impolite awakening".

After being knowledgeable by way of the use of Crawford, Weir, who've grow to be the officer assigned to this incident, stated he had replied to that cope with earlier this 12 months.

Weir said he had first met at 15 January 1970 and were made aware about abnormal activities said thru the tenants of a terrific condominium.

There have been opinions of loud noises and odd happenings.

Since his first go to, Weir said he contacted the engineering branch of St. Catharines, who inspected the building and discovered no structural harm in the constructing.

The gas employer emerge as moreover referred to as with the entire heating tool inspected and water and the whole thing labored well and in specific state of affairs even as respecting the normal jogging specifications.

The police even bled heat water warmers, but the noises persisted, due to the truth the normal sports of devices transferring through manner of unseen forces inside the rental.

Weir stated that at the identical time as he supports Crawford sooner or later of the selection "family dispute" February 6, 1970, on the equal time as he became in the condo, he observed several trophies bowling be disposed one after the alternative on a timber board on top of a radiator.

He additionally stated that he positioned the wall clock within the kitchen disconnect landing at the ground with out a legitimate.

The police who've been on the scene at the night time time of 6 February 1970 stated that the "agent" or "host" of poltergeist hobby defined have emerge as the eleven 12 months antique son of the complainant.

Crawford said that when the 11 three hundred and sixty five days antique boy went through the apartment, the snap shots on the wall, "threw inside the same way that a dog wags its tail whilst it's miles glad to look his draw close."

The officials say that all the invisible stress pushed the boy in the direction of the wall severa instances and moreover they declare that the boy changed into sitting on a large, heavy chair.

the chair grew to become round itself, pinning the child at the ground.

The chair become so heavy that it took human beings to decorate the chair.

The officers additionally said that a Chesterfield, protecting four people, levitated to about eighteen centimeters from the floor.

One of the ladies sitting at the sofa dwindled on the identical time as she determined that she come to be sitting on a table levitated.

Weir said the child have become sitting on the knee of a policeman at the identical time as invisible entity attempted to take the child.

It took the electricity of officers to maintain the kid at the knee wherein he become sitting.

The officers additionally noticed the children's mattress levitate the ground of the room and watch the worried infant jumping from the bed

They grew to emerge as their attention to the concerned little one and after they lower back to the spot in which the bed become, the mattress modified into about toes off the floor, supported thru two chairs.

Dolls and pics fell from the walls.

Chapter 9: A Desk Lamp Within The Chamber Has Fallen

A large heavy chest end up moving far from the wall and got here again.

A chair in the a ways nook of the room rose into the air and slammed to the ground.

The first-class gadgets that remained within the rental and that were now not laid low with the invisible forces of poltergeist were a crucifix and an image of the Virgin Mary with a palm leaf on the body.

The police requested the kid's father to make arrangements for children to spend the night time time somewhere else.

When youngsters began out to get dressed to go away the condo, library fell.

The 11 12 months antique boy left home to live collectively with her grandmother.

I proper proper here have been unsubstantiated evaluations that poltergeist pastime endured together with his grandmother.

According to Bill Weir, the poltergeist lasted 28 days - a whole lunar cycle.

Scotland

Edinburgh 1999

Greyfriars Cemetery

The most haunting-the-global

This cemetery can be very broadly recognized to tourists, probable because of the story of Bobby canine, a Skye Terrier who end up immortalized with the useful aid of Disney. Bobby belonged to John Gray, a night time time time policeman who labored in Edinburgh, they had been inseparable.

One day John died of tuberculosis and became buried in Greyfriars cemetery.

Bobby - who died fourteen years after spent the relaxation of his existence lying near the grave of his late preserve close. It is likewise the resting vicinity of the famous Scottish poet William McGonagall who has the recognition of being the worst poet inside the information of the United Kingdom.

This place seems to fascinate people and loads of humans revel in atypical emotions even as they are there, despite the truth that they will be now not straight away visible manifestation of a witness.

Unfortunately, this cemetery inspires moreover normally a incredible deal people nowadays:

In 2004, teens are responsible of desecration.

They had reduce off the top of one of the corpses and used as a puppet.

Historically, this cemetery is referred to as the 7th century cemetery in which "bloody" George Mackenzie - the persecutor of the Covenanters - have become buried.

Since it's far the scene of many haunting and amazing appearances, such as George virtually ghost himself, the well-known Mackenzie poltergeist.

The ghost of Mackenzie (Mackenzie Poltergeist)

George Mackenzie become born in Dundee in 1636 and changed proper into a prison professional throughout the reign of Charles II.

He odious strategies and persecuted Covenanters torturing and allowing them to die, which earned him the nickname Bloody Mackenzie.

He died in 1691 and became buried in Greyfriars cemetery wherein, ironically, some of his sufferers died.

He become buried in a big mausoleum flashy and stated that because of all the horrible subjects that a whole lot in his existence, he ought to in no manner rested in peace.

it's far following the desecration of the tomb inside the past due 1990s that "Poltergeist" (Poltergeist) might also need to make his.

The poltergeist in query emerge as named "Mackenzie" due to an incident befell in the mausoleum simply in advance than the ghost in query is not placed to react.

This tale even been stated thru using the BBC which can also furthermore show extreme.

December 1998:

The gates of the cemetery of Greyfriars which can be typically closed at night time time time had been open that day, probably due to an oversight.

Seeing the doors open, a homeless who sought safe haven from the rain entered the cemetery and wandered for a second earlier than breaking into the mausoleum of Mackenzie.

He possibly selected this one as it became one of the tombs of the cemetery that modified into great capable of guard him.

Looking through the gates, he must have seen a slight in the backside of the mausoleum.

Intrigued, he then climbed over the gates and observed a small starting within the lower again of the tomb wherein he need to pass.

Once interior, he decided a staircase that induced in which we had the our our bodies.

There also are determined numerous coffin and opened one with the useful resource of pronouncing that there can be some thing of charge buried with the frame.

Meanwhile, and however the past due hour, a person modified into walking his canine within the cemetery.

He heard the noise made thru the homeless searching for to open the coffin and headed for Mackenzie's grave to look what it modified into.

At that point, the homeless would possibly have fallen via a hole in the ground and will be landing in a pit complete of skeletons. Terrified, he left the tomb ran.

Man taking walks his dog notion it was the ghost of Mackenzie and fled screaming.

The perceiving, without safe haven believed he became pursuing someone or some aspect and screamed greater lovely.

Following this incident, the metropolis of Edinburgh determined to shut the mausoleum and the birthday celebration or come to be the Covenanters Prison this is now available thru the ghost tower.

This incident seems to have woke up the ghost of Mackenzie due to the fact while you bear in mind that that night time time time, greater than 4 hundred assaults have been mentioned, 100 seventy people vanished with out counting the variety of lights and unexplained drafts and vain animals that have been determined there .

Despite numerous attacks may take place, the poltergeist become in no manner seen, so it isn't feasible to apprehend if it is truly that of Mackenzie.

France

 Joigny (Yonne branch)

Early 11th century

According to the monk chronicler Raoul Glaber.

"At the same time a amazing omen and worth to find out vicinity here manifested near the citadel of Joigny, with a noble guy named Arlebaud.

For three years, he fell almost continuously for the duration of the house, the stones of diverse sizes, which can still be seen heaps all round his house.

They came from the air, or they penetrated through the roof?

This is what you could although say.

What is sure is that this rain, which stopped neither night time nor day, do no longer damage one individual, and no longer even broke a vase. "

" many people recognized among the ones stones restrict (terminals) in their fields.

It additionally changed into in that were made there of roads, homes and severa houses within the distance, or theneighborhood. "

"This prodigy brought a disaster on the own family ofArlebaudSince that fast after disputes broke out in opposition to their buddies in 1017, the Knights of Auxerre inside the carrier of Earl Landry about the land of Going, within the county of Sens, which he had taken, which degenerate into battle at harvest time, and plenty of own family contributors ofArlebaud had been killed whilst they desired to take their land.

Later, quarrels commenced out another time after each unique 30 years and taken on new murders within the equal family. "

this narrative is placed as an unexplained case poltergeist.

La Fontaine Raoul Glaber in Moutiers en Puisaye.

The monk Raoul Glaber, nicknamed columnist, one thousand, one of the best chroniclers of the Middle Ages, who spent numerous years with the monks of the Monastery of Moutiers among a thousand and 1047, the 365 days he died.

Paris 1846

We are in November 1846 in Paris, in a house placed along the Rue Racine.

This house modified into bombed every night thru stones of all sizes fuck doors, domestic home windows and roof.

The proprietor of the residence, Mr. Lerrible, a complaint believing the victim of an unbalanced.

In all, he'll record 30 lawsuits within the course of X.

Monitoring sellers are located earlier than the house, the police commissioner is going there.

A platoon of the 24th regiment of hunters even dispatched with out outcomes.

Never can we find out character who throws stones at the residence.

then logs seized of the case brought on a stir.

Three months after the primary stone throwing, the phenomenon stops .

They accuse Mr. Lerrible have the whole thing plotted.

The latter defends and assigns the newspaper that circulated this lie for defamation.

He will win the lawsuit.

During the discussions, it modified into not stated the arrest of a perpetrator. Asked with the aid of a researcher, the response of changing the police commissioner modified into furthermore unambiguous:

"Mr. Commissioner of Police confirm you need me, sir, that regardless of our tireless research, we may additionally moreover want to never discover some detail, and I can assure you in advance that we are able to by no means discover a few element! "

Paris rue Racine

 Thee mill Perbet

Between Laussonne and Saint-Front (department Haute-Loire)

1902

The foundation of the statistics become in December 1902. On the way to Laussonne taking walks three valiantly return farmers marketplace.

Then they pay interest crying and screaming up the mill, nestled inside the center of nowhere.

Listening simplest to their courage, they decide to move there. The three guys will find out in those places a regular haunting scene of what's now called the poltergeist.

The daughters of the miller, and Mary Philomena, aged 12 and 14, have the eyes rolling and are prey to paranormal phenomenon.

They are thrown inside the air for no motive, and dragged along the floor thru way of an unseen pressure.

All round them the factors rage inside the residence:

crockery shatters and breaks on the same time as overturning furnishings.

Blankets go away the mattress rooms and could cowl the cows within the robust many witnesses declare to have visible.

Despite their efforts, the farmers are not capable of manage the women.

A shoe is thrown in opposition to a tile like magic and breaks.

A stone coming back from outdoor breaks every other tile.

One of the key farmers explained that she have become burning.

The mill attracts crowds and journalists

In the instances that followed the ones occasions, masses of human beings went to the farm to attend the activities.

The story goes that a lot of them in the long run had to depart, due to the fact many items of the residence fell on them, moved through an invisible, evil strain.

Curious received at the pinnacle soaps, stones, shoes ...

These sports are first-class stopped while the two women, that people had dubbed "the daughters of the satan", left the mill to Paris.

The case, but, added on a stir and made headlines inside the nearby and countrywide press.

There emerge as, particularly, posted in The Future of the Haute-Loire and in particular the presence of newshounds from London and Belgium to relate events.

A postcard had even been edited.

Postcard: the group to peer the mill "haunted"

Here is a document of the time published:

ECHO OF WONDERFUL

Some transcription errors may additionally additionally appear within the text

A HAUNTED HOUSE

On steep grooves of Aubépin, tributary Gagne, the bottom of a most picturesque valley changed into decided a mill known as Perbet whose monotonous ticking definitely appeared not particular to draw evil spirits and serve Theater to the exploits of a ghost occult presently the dice easy all conversations in the evenings our cottages Vellaves :

However it comes dice to seem in this small mill isolated dice habitation, a few incidents that could alter titled worry those who suppose rightly that the manifestations of the beyond are viable.

There are about eight facts Joubert Etienne mill owner in question out of place his spouse known as Mary Exbrayat.

Rubber sucker had children and he may also want to simplest control; its manufacturing is remaria- with a maid Marie Boyer.

It regarded that the union needed to: be much less

 and that the general public in no way would have to worry about swimming-reliance while there approximately a yr, it became said the advent of ghosts at the mill.

It even claimed that Mary had appeared to Exbrayat Joubert Stephen and their daughter, fourteen years.

These supernatural activities observed no massive debt. It regarded them: forgotten, if lé Thursday, November 27th, statistics as a minimum extremely good had now not come motive consternation in the localities surrounding ..

That day at approximately 3 o'clock, three farmers: Masson Jean Pierre and Sahuè Gerentes Claude, it alderman of Saint-Front, passed thru using the mill Perbet coming back from the marketplace Laussonne.

They had been very amazed to pay attention the weeping and cries of terror coming from in the house.

They stopped to pay attention higher.

At this time, Marie Boyer, married his 2nd; wedding ceremony Joubert seemed on the door and referred to as for assist.

The three men entered, believing that their intervention would possibly there peace in the family, a 2nd under talk.

It might be hard to painting the amazement of terrible humans while, inside the kitchen, in which they entered, they determined the fixtures overturned and transported from one corner to every other of the apartment, kitchen utensils, dishes, splintered , children jostled and thrown violently to the floor, at the same time as within the barn, adjacent to the kitchen, cows, mysteriously covered with sheets and blankets, bellowed and struggled ...Jean Masson, a lot much less surprised than his partners, Joubert then asked the lady (husband no longer being

 there), who suggested him that the writer of this noise, mysterious can be that Mary Exbrayat the primary

 spouse of Joubert, and the day earlier than it had tested its presence with a letter that have been positioned on a table and an look which had witnessed the eldest daughter who's fourteen years.

Masson may additionally want to then recognize the force

 occult and hustled everyone and each trouble. He attempted to preserve a little one in her fingers.

He found out with horror that she changed into pulled violently, and this in one of these way that one of the shoes of the girl become abducted and thrown towards the window which he broke a tile.

 So exceeded Thursday midnight.

 On Friday, the same phenomena befell.

The priest have grow to be referred to as but his exorcisms had been not

 any shape of impact.

 In the night time time from Saturday to Sunday a few; courageous residents resolved to sleep at the mill to look what is virtually happening.

Woe took because of the fact within the midnight, they have been placed up.

Stones, footwear and cleansing cleaning soap to quantities fell on their heads without them whence they came and screwed them the noait.

Sunday the whole thing had stopped.

ULYSSES CAP.

Our colleague Awakening of the Haute-Loire of 6 December

recounts the case:

Phenomena of a supernatural order, we used such sports activities to keep to account "The rapper Spirit" took place numerous instances, for added than a 12 months in a residence known as Mill Perbet, inhabited through the appointed Etienne Joubert, miller and his circle of relatives.

They may have spent about if disregarded, ultimate week, for 3 consecutive days, they have been reproduced and, with the aid in their nature incredible-depth, had thrown a stir in surrounding groups.

Here are the maximum unsdes records, which highlights witnesses had been named:

he Masson Jean Sahuc Gerentes Pierre and Jean-Claude j latter councilor, populace of the vicinity Bournac, metropolis of Saint-Front.

Last Thursday, November 27, approximately 3 o'clock, the 3 guys had again Laussonne marketplace whilst arrived on the residence of Joubert who modified into on their manner, they have been surprised to listen: weeping and cries terror coming from inside the residence They have been no longer arrested Marie Boyer, companion, 2d wife Etienne Joubert, regarded on her doorstep and called for assist.

It might be difficult to portray their amazement at the same time as, entered the kitchen inside the center of a hellish Din, they noticed the furniture overturned and transported from one region to a few different of the apartment; the cube kitchen utensils, crockery, splintered, broken thru stones thrown via an invisible hand; kids themselves, pushed and thrown vivement- ashore while at the stables adjoining the cooked, cows, die mysteriously protected sheets and blankets offense, bellowed and struggled; and all this noise going on without any damage to anybody.

One of the three beginners, Jean Masson, with the resource of coming some time to conquer the fear that gripped him, asked the female Joubert (For the husband, for worse, have turn out to be that day absent) of what 'she idea of all this upheaval.

This, as may be understood, in a broken voice, answered that the culprit of maximum of those sounds became named Mary Exbrayat, the first partner of her husband, who died there about 8 years, which had manifested its presence through a letter she had deposited at the desk there in advance than and which had not held counted it, after which she had been in my view with considered certainly one of his daughters, aged fourteen, complaining of terrible execution of his will.

In those few terms, the kids persevered to roll on the floor, driven, they said, by way of the use of an invisible hand.

Jean Masson said, intrigued consequently takes the maximum critical head immediately to attempt to preserve and realizes with horror that she is strongly drawn with the aid of way of an invisible pressure, and this so that one of the shoes the lady is abducted and violently thrown within the direction of the window:

he breaks a tile, and on the identical 2d, a stone from the outside and breaking each other window, surely energy at his toes.

We decide redoubled his fright even as taking hand that stone, he reveals that it's miles heat.

So exceeded Thursday night time; and, at night time time time, the 3 witnesses of those normal scenes withdrew into a rustic of mind that it isn't tough to conce-see.

The husband again come to be forced to desert the house for the night.

The subsequent day, Friday, the noise die these kind of objects had spread unexpectedly, close by residents got here to appearance the ones uncommon phenomena, and people who entered the house have been greeted through way of stones or other projectiles mysteriously.

Only lé Saturday morning that the ones noises ceased.

It says he stays exceptional that the deceased could have regarded Exbrayat Marie Joubert and Stephen antique daughter die fourteen, whom she could probably have communicated his intentions.

The priest of Laussonne, we had felt himself obliged to call, went within the residence at some stage in the day on Saturday.

Farm Saint-Jeans-of-Maurienne (Savoie department)

1955

This case is a magical episode that many burdened Maurienne 60 years in the beyond.

On February 25, 1955 in fact the dishes and furniture began to fly in an vintage house within the College Street.

An exorcist have end up known as, but the holy water that stopped nicely short time the sarabande.

People depended on witnessed many activities that afflicted them.

After a few weeks the agitation fell, but the case had stirred many.

Photography poltergeist type phenomena, which might have been taken into 1955 on a farm Saint-Jeans-of-Maurienne.

Haunted sanatorium clinical medical doctor Cuénot Arcachon (Gironde)

1963

00046.Jpeg

These phenomena have rarely lasted extra than 4 months, from mid-May 1963 until the begin of September of the identical yr.

At first people who've been "sufferers" positioned it proper down to pranksters and renounced to bitch for fear of "reprisals".

He changed into now not going an afternoon with out some inpatients, maximum mendacity on automobiles, placed themselves the aim of bullets of any awesome.

It could be insignificant, the size of a gravel than half of of -brique.

But in no way, these stones will harm, if best not frequently and definitely lightly.

Soon, a few had been opened by way of way of way of the health center team of workers, first it changed into belief some phantasmagoria of some patients.

It's just that in early August the Director of Personnel have become notified of this collection of incidents.

In this time c language, the sick, have end up suspicious and started to test the facts and gestures of a resident on the sanatorium, named Angelina, which seemed to the "victim" desired of these phenomena.

But he left the hooked up order, on 7 July 1963 did not trade the state of affairs.

Rather, he appears to have carried over a woman of 17 years, Jacqueline R ...

Photo Jacqueline alleged. 1 September 1963

Obviously, it become she who emerge as now below stated Robert Tocquet.

All he had to discover a touch while in any place out of doors terraces for the stones begin to fall in its course.

If she abstained from the medical institution, the stone throwing stopped.

When she reappeared, they resumed after a latency of 5 to 10 minutes each time.

Sometimes stones jets had been interrupted for several days to resume a greater lovable in electricity and volume.

One night time a few sick accrued the stones fell spherical him, placed them in a pile subsequent to his room, making plans to reveal the next day at Robert Tocquet.

The next morning the hobby changed into lengthy gone.

We asked the residence responsibilities and patients connecting rooms, no person recalled seeing those stones piled For people who although doubt the magical phenomenon of those sports, Robert Tocquet cites 3 separate instances that no rational cause of deciphering .

"One day in August, even as the stones fell in abundance at the north terrace, unwell, MT Andre police officer in Paris, seemed up at the appropriate 2nd a large stone, about 200 to 3 hundred grams, became launched through the open window of a chamber of the second one; ground of the building element is decommissioned.

He located no fingers, no head, no one, but saw handiest a rock protruding of stated window to fall to the ground commits if run from the once more of the room by using someone hiding.

Upstairs proper away explored, turn out to be found empty and the door of that room locked as all unused rooms.

"Another night time, spherical 21 pm, 3 sufferers were at the terrace with Jacqueline R. While stone throwing started out once more, manifestly despite the fact that coming from the same constructing.

To have the coronary heart internet, the four friends went up to the 1/three ground, opened the door upstairs locked from out of doors and observed no man or woman. Back down on the terrace, the stones maintain to fall, they went remember this time the second one floor in which all the doorways of the rooms have been also closed, latches removed.

For the second time, their technique have end up unsuccessful even after taking the trouble to open every piece with an emergency latch.

Some day, even as MC became lying on the north terrace of his car, stones rained down in such quantity that, desirous approximately anger, he cried out in the wings:

there are enough, that idiot can not it prevent!

Immediately rockfall stopped and did no longer resume timidly 1/2 of of an hour later.

Another witness said that a day while the climate turn out to be especially beautiful, all patients, not excepting one, down from their room to spend the afternoon at the terrace.

That day, it come to be missing or a affected person or a frame of humans member, and, ever, there were such lots of stones thrown, that could result in the conviction of all that no ill nor any member group of workers couldn't be suspected.

Shortly before the stone-throwing phenomena completely surrender, a few sufferers needed to go through to be wakened unnecessarily at night time time through violent blows toward the door of their room.

Never, we couldn't rent absolutely everyone to be the author.

Robert Tocquet himself witnessed those repeated undesirable outcomes.

In its conclusions, the expert admits the paranormal nature of what end up positioned and finds it not feasible to offer an reason for them through normal interpretation factors.

Subsequently, Dr. Cuénot sold his medical institution; Later, the building modified into destroyed.

The "wall that speaks" Common Machine

(Department of Nièvre) 1973

Chapter 11: Dominique, Communicating With The Poltergeist

The life of a small own family have become very disturbed discovered shot thru the manifestation of a poltergeist, who had hit the wall of Dominica chamber, the boy's circle of relatives.

Every night time around 20h, brilliant drumming modified into heard ... In order that the little boy had grown aware of touch the poltergeist who answered simplest through using rapping into the wall.

A few days later, the family decided to touch community Police Brigade, to strive to research more about this bizarre phenomenon.

The case modified into followed very considerably through Warrant Officer Bernard Guilbert, who at the time become commander of the Brigade of La Machine.

So he went to the scene, with a tape recorder. For fifteen minutes, now not a few component came about, even as all at once shots had been hit in the course of the wall and were recorded through the digicam.

This glaringly made a excellent noise, a lot that Machinois and different curious, once in a while from very a protracted manner, went to massive range in the house that regarded haunted.

Now retired, Bernard although recalls thoroughly the phenomenon:

"The tale seems surreal, a poltergeist pat on the wall of the room of a teen and he responds nicely to particular questions.

I observed severa times the phenomenon, and I in my view have cited with the thoughts.

He modified into requested arrivals trifecta, he has given some other place. He have become additionally capable of punctuate military marches or songs of Marie Laforet.

He spoke back non-public questions I asked him. So that become definitely unsettling. My gendarmes, but, disturbed.

Inevitably, we completed a intense studies. It emerge as hideouts. Gendarmes have been positioned everywhere, at the floor, in the once more of the partition, within the basement, inside the garden. Nothing, there has been not anything. I am effective of 1 component, there has been no trick, no deception. "

All additives of the residence have been scrutinized, however no deception have become detected.

Even extra tremendous:

the police need to touch the poltergeist and conversation grow to be mounted and showed.

The poltergeist knew the form of kids of one of the gendarmes gift at the scene, the amount of cartridges in the gun it (even as he himself did no longer apprehend it), and the shape of policemen present on the brigade's Machine.

Incredibly, the blows continuously correspond to actual numbers, which were occasionally unknown with the useful resource of the protagonists themselves!

The police say that when they positioned their hands to a distance of approximately 40cm from the the the front, they though felt the surprise wave that unfold!

The teen, who took it as a exercise, amused even humming songs simply so the poltergeist make the rhythm thing.

He brazenly questioned him, to check him.

Making irony evidence, it's going to even ask the spirit to are searching ahead to her future trifecta winner ...

Men and women have attempted to touch the poltergeist.

Obviously, scientists went on internet net web page to attempt to find rational reasons for all this, however in no way in a feature to expose that it modified into most effective a trivial deception.

Some passage charlatans, even tried to abuse the credulity of the own family, but it changed into no longer relying on Warrant Guilbert, who hastened to "smooth".

For no motive, the phenomenon ceased mysteriously, December thirteen, 1973.

Yves Lignon (Mathematician and diagnosed Parapsychologist), have become contacted through the Gendarmerie, to try and remedy this case.

For him, it's far smooth:

it's far absolutely a real paranormal phenomenon which responds, consequently, to any rational clarification ... But not a few factor become ever proved.

There remains no scientific concept that would apprehend this phenomenon.

More than forty years later, the thriller of the house is continuously whole.

However, it modified into an uplifting experience for the Gendarmes because it modified into the primary time they had been dealing with this kind of phenomenon, as a part of an studies ... And it come to be moreover the first time they have been making sound recordings of a magical event.

The former proprietors of this residence have moved to the south, exhausted with the resource of these sports activities and the enthusiasm they procured.

They desired to stay anonymous, to overlook this records and be capable of lead a peaceful lifestyles.

Romania

Eleanor Zugun 1913-1998

GIRL ROMANIAN POLTERGEIST

It's been about 90 years Zugun Eleanor, a more youthful woman from Romania, have turn out to be the maximum decided poltergeist, studied and examined the 20 th century.

The poltergeist worrying phenomena that have persevered in the course of Europe make the case one of the maximum splendid attested.

It is likewise the first poltergeist instances in which Freudian psychoanalysis has been implemented.

The American researcher D. Scott Rogo considered the concept of a "sexual basis for poltergeist ... Turned into simplest recommended with the useful resource of the usage of the case of Zugun".

So, he helped cement the link amongst adolescence and poltergeist pastime is a great connection made nowadays.

The case started out in 1925 at the same time as violent poltergeist erupted spherical Eleanor Zugun, then aged eleven, after a dispute collectively together along with her grandmother in some unspecified time in the future of a go to.

The home of his grandmother became hit with the useful resource of a tub of stones, smashing home windows.

Inside small devices commenced flying spherical Eleanor.

She turned into rapid decrease again to her mother and father in Talpa.

Arriving on the house, the demonstrations continued, terrifying his father and stepmother.

Fearing that the evil forces are at art work, Eleanor changed into provided to the nearby priest, who attended the demonstrations.

A jug of water rose into the air and a heavy trunk swayed Eleanor short after it have become seated.

The subsequent night time, a trunk has been seen to move Nicolai Ostafi.

Shortly after a board to mix the boiled rose and hit Ostafi on the top, inflicting a wound.

An exorcism didn't quell protests and Eleanor changed into despatched to the small monastery of the eighteenth century Govorei to desire.

The phenomena persisted unabated.

She modified into then transferred to a psychiatric sanatorium for adults, apparently after media coverage of sports and concerns approximately his treatment.

The media insurance has attracted the eye of German newspapers that caused the go to of the German psychic researcher Fritz Grunewald Berlin.

He traveled to Talpa and positioned Eleanor and will locate no fault in it.

He purported to pursue the problem but unluckily Grunewald died all at once of a coronary coronary coronary heart attack with the useful aid of creating a short circulate again to Berlin.

Fortunately, if Eleanor have become taken up with the aid of a incredible younger Austrian aristocrat, Countess Zoe Wassilko-Serecki (1897-1966) who spoke Romanian.

In September 1925, the Countess started out to Talpa the course of the deceased Herr Grunwald, funded through using the most influential determine of the German psychic research, Baron Schrenck-Notzing.

She controlled to touch Eleanor and her circle of relatives and determined to take Eleanor Austria.

After having paid cash to the father and stepmother Eleanor, Countess received permission to head away the lady of the peasant family surroundings and convey alongside aspect her to Vienna for research.

He turn out to be no longer rushed - Eleanor ultimately arrived in Vienna January 29, 1926.

Countess Eleonore right now moved into his condo, allowing him to stay there for months underneath the close to supervision of the Countess and psychic researchers.

PHENOMENON CONTINUES

Often, the separation of the home surroundings appears to cease phenomena.

However, this doesn't display up.

The arrival of Eleanor in Vienna changed into fast marked through a modern-day day poltergeist pastime.

The first incident modified into the autumn of a silver spoon reported via a housekeeper; Countess to begin with had doubts approximately how this passed off, displaying that she could not be fooled with the resource of the usage of the young Eleanor.

More annoying for the family became transferring an ink pot, thrown for the duration of the room spraying and smearing appreciably with the content fabric fabric.

Following this, all of the ink modified into blocked and Eleanor moves have been restrained to advantageous additives of the condo. Water mysteriously crammed the boots of Eleanor.

Noting that the phenomena usually came about inside the identical room or in a far off part of Eleanor and figuring out that damage to valuables within the apartment would possibly have a observe if Eleanor modified into inner collect, Countess spoke back thru restricting his movements therefore the living room and the consuming room and some bedrooms had been off limits.

This left the corridor with Eleanor and servants quarters.

The poltergeist phenomena determined Eleanor and emblems appearing on his pores and skin. The sports were attributed to Eleanor entity called "Dracu" the Romanian phrase for satan.

The end result have become one of the closest and longest studies of a teen on the center of an endemic of Poltergeist.

'Dracu'

Chapter 12: Scratches On The Face Of Eleanor

Of path, the choice "Dracu" at once evokes the account immortal vampire Dracula and Bram Stoker.

Today, a youngster who talks approximately a vampiric entity that bites can be visible as passionate about the romantic and erotic photographs of vampires in fiction, cinema and television.

This modified into no longer the case of Eleanor thinking about, in 1926, the cult of the immortal vampire, in big part targeted on film, had no longer regarded as a social phenomenon - Bela Lugosi had ever bitten anyone on degree or in 'display.

But 'Dracu' Eleonore shared an unpleasant feature associated with the fictional vampire - he preferred to chunk a more youthful woman - with Eleanor, his most effective decided on victim.

Bite marks, punctures and abrasions began acting on his pores and pores and skin and were photographed.

Much has been registered with the aid of the use of the Countess Wassilko such as:

Raps on furniture "contributions" of toys and precise items falling from the air in numerous rooms in the apartment.

Movements of items, along with furnishings.

Automatic writing produced with the aid of Eleonore.

Disappearance and reappearance of gadgets, every so often for weeks.

On one event, a bizarre voice.

surprising motion of needles observed in the hands and Eleanor of arms.

The devices were moved and appeared to materialize and dematerialize.

Locked doors do no longer seem to limit transportation.

These blanketed three factors fails legitimate a set owned through the daddy of the Countess; they reappeared after 3 days seeming fall from the air.

The Countess recorded all phenomena, first in his handwritten logbooks, Vol. I - III, totaling 141 pages an awesome manner to remodel later into a ebook.

In flat rotations web site visitors to the apartment taking turns keeping the paper prepared through the countess. A common of extra than three thousand phenomena nearly 9 hundred are nicely documented.

The Countess has recorded 67 incidents in in the future, and 1,050 in 3 months, even as Eleanor have become in Vienna.

The British researcher Harry Price (1881-1948) believed to have witnessed each dermal phenomena and object movement for the duration of his visit to the rental of the countess, in Vienna, in which a replicate turned into mysteriously transported with disruptions repeated books in the apartment of the countess.

The movement of gadgets has often shifted almost really to the "dermal phenomena," that is to say, scratches and bites on his pores and pores and skin and coughing, so there were truly top notch degrees.

The frame of Eleanor suffered marks, scratches and bites apparent that regarded on his pores and skin and that had been attributed to attacks by way of using the invisible 'Dracu.

The chew marks did now not match the teeth smooth Eleonore one that changed into accountable for the bites, it come to be not Eleanor who inflicted them.

Some punctures left footprints like teeth inside the pores and skin that Eleanor have become stained, it seemed like saliva.

On 25 October 1926, Eleanor became tested thru a number of scientific doctors in Berlin and a zoologist who examined the "saliva" acting across the bites.

It have become located that the substance is whole of microorganisms distinct from those discovered in the mouth of Eleanor, although there has been a doubt as to whether or not or now not or now not he became coughing.

Swarms in the white don't forget range were staphylococci bacteria, associated with numerous infections.

The case of scratches and abrasions poltergeist are recorded historically but significantly scattered in the literature of poltergeist.

For instance, in September 1910 a poltergeist biting / nipping / putting in Turffontein, South Africa, became filmed. He moved devices and left "nail marks" on the arm of a sixteen three hundred and sixty five days vintage female.

In fall 1926, the countess embarked with Eleanor for a "tour" of a few 5 months, journeying the primary psychic researchers of the time, masking London, Berlin, Nuremberg and Munich.

Harry Price has tested Eleanor, and a number of scientists and observers interested by his arrival in London, receiving hundreds of exposure.

Eleanor became the problem of a have a look at on the National Laboratory for Psychical Research, which added approximately a detailed report and a big insurance inside the British press.

Besides the flat tires, there was additionally the stigmatic marks and marks at the breasts and wrists Eleanor.

Brands and psychosomatic lesions have been located within the case of hysterical sufferers and stigma, however the marks and abrasions on Eleanor seemed like being physically inflicted via manner of an outdoor stress.

However, constant with subsequent evaluations Eleanor had extremely touchy pores and skin.

Eleanor appeared to maintain a exquisite childlike amazing Although moody at instances, it seems to be a smooth and as an possibility exquisite toddler.

The undeveloped nature of the personality of Eleanor "it changed into more like an 8 of a little one." thirteen

Eleanor regarded as just like the Countess, irrespective of the reality that this could have been the attachment of a toddler who had in no way referred to loads of hobby thus far.

She did no longer show altered states of attention that often regarded to rise up in times of poltergeist, and the thriller of what lay behind the bodily symptoms and symptoms remained.

At the save you of the excursion in 1927, a file of dermographiques phenomena Eleanor come to be carried out on a film 36 mm.

The countess desired the movie to be tested most effective on the subject of his introductory text.

It is silent and watch the periods collectively along with her finished via 3 investigators, a female and men wherein reputedly seem abrasions of the pores and pores and pores and skin. In the give up, this is a worrying movie.

The phenomena declined after Eleanor reached puberty and started out to menstruate, after ceasing surely. With the Supreme phenomena, Countess Eleonore funded in order that it reasons as a hairdresser and she or he ended up yet again in Romania.

Chapter 13: Poltergeist, The Darkish Issue Of The Paranormal

The global has existed considering the truth that factor immemorial. It occurs right subsequent to us, even though it is tough for us to absolutely take delivery of that this kind of trouble may be actual. No one is privy to how the number one human beings understood and described it, but possibly that 7,000-twelve months-old corpse, located in Bulgaria, over which a huge stone were positioned, may additionally need to shed moderate on historical ideals in evil spirits . It is terrifying, arguable, black and incomprehensible. In a word... Poltergeist .

What is excellent approximately an intense paranormal phenomenon, which includes the poltergeist, is that it has manifested itself in all cultures of the area , from the start beneath, strictly, the same characteristics.

People who couldn't recognize each distinct, describe identical scary testimonies, and this not from the day prior to this or today, however due to the fact historical instances.

Perhaps the earliest written thing out of a poltergesic phenomenon comes from the number one century AD, on the same time as the Roman historian of Jewish basis, Flavius Titus, mentions times of "possession" and "haunting" , in terms identical to those who describe in recent times poltergeist sports.

Jacob Grimm, one of the famous Brothers Grimm, describes in his Deutsche Mythologie , an extensive treatise on Germanic myths and legends, a series of everyday poltergeist cases.

The excellent regarded is the most effective that took place in Bingen-am-Rhein, inside the yr 305, whilst in the house of a community humans commenced to be lifted inside the air, thrown faraway from bed and violently hit with the beneficial aid of an unseen pressure.

The reminiscences of the time claim that the stones rose on their very own and had been thrown to passers-through with the aid of the use of manner of an invisible hand, even as people who dared to method, the identical stress tore their clothes. All this time, loud noises and noisy voices of those who couldn't be visible may be heard within the residence affected by the mysterious phenomena.

In his adventure spherical Wales in 1191, the chronicler priest Giraldus Cambrensis cited in his big paintings, Itinerarium Cambriae , an occasion he can also need to never forget approximately about.

He claims that "unclean spirits" had determined an area in a house in Pembrokeshire , and that they had been throwing dust and tough gadgets at close by human beings. Moreover, the "spirits" addressed the astonished witnesses and, greater than once, found to the name of the game crowd the intimate lives of a number of the ones gift.

No a good deal much less famous is the case of the "Tedworth Drummer" in England in 1661.

The incident turn out to be said through using the truth seeker Joseph Glanvill inside the work Saducismus Triumphatus , and refers to the terrifying sports that befell after the arrest of a vagabond drummer. Accused of acquiring cash with the aid of manner of flawed way, the drummer have become imprisoned and his drum turn out to be confiscated. It become simplest the begin of the nightmare for the populace of the small medieval agreement.

Immediately after the arrest, in the end of the night time time, human beings started out to pay interest the loud sounds of the drum, despite the fact that nobody must see the only causing the terrible noise, and the mysterious manifestations lasted for weeks on give up.

And if we upload to those sports the only from 1817, called "the haunting of Bell's witch", an in any other case well-known case in the United States, we will only complete a depressing photograph of the poltergeist phenomena in information.

Numerous eyewitnesses testified that at John William Bell Sr.'s farm in Tennessee, a sequence of unexplained activities came about in the yr of grace 1817.

It all started out even as Bell Sr. Met an unseen animal of large stature. He had the body of a canine and the top of a rabbit, and managed to break out in advance than being caught in the arms via the farmer. Immediately after this meeting, the voices of unseen creatures started to be heard night after night time time time .

The "spirits" laughed gloomily and attacked the people who got here to visit the farm. Eventually, they ceased on the time of the mysterious demise of John William Bell Sr. A bottle containing an unknown liquid became determined close to his inert frame.

Tested on the own family cat, the liquid proved to be an extremely robust and speedy poison. Nobody is privy to who gave the bottle to the farmer or how he have become satisfied to drink its contents.

Poltergeist inside the twentieth century

1972. Thorton Hearth, England. One of the most frightening instances of a poltergeist ever recorded come to be to take region in the home of a circle of relatives of small English industrialists .

It all started out in August of that yr, 1972.

It changed into beyond midnight while the individuals of the circle of relatives in query had been woke up by means of manner of the deafening noise of the radio, which had apparently commenced on its very non-public and, similarly, had changed its frequency to that of a remote places station. The odd incident became followed through the autumn of the lampshade of one of the lamps within the residence. Just weird coincidences, the owners knowledgeable themselves. However, the same occasions started out to be repeated regularly.

The radio have become on for the duration of the night because the lampshade began out to jump farther and farther via the room. It changed into simply the start of phenomena that could closing for almost four years.

 The occasions worsened at Christmas of the equal 365 days. The terrified family described how the wintry weather tree began out out to shake violently, shaken as despite the fact that by means of way of an unseen entity, and an ornament flew thru the room hitting one of the circle of relatives participants.

From that day on, uncommon footsteps and voices began out to be heard inside the rooms wherein no character want to were. The doorways slammed open, slammed into the partitions, and the light bulbs in the house came on and rancid with out anyone switching at the switches.

The pals of the circle of relatives helplessly witnessed the drama of those within the residence and proposed to them to name more clergymen to bless their domestic. But this simplest made matters worse.

In the presence of severa witnesses, along with cops, clergymen or perhaps newshounds, the terrifying phenomena continued. The chair wherein one of the policemen have come to be status rose with him in the air, then collapsed

on the floor.

Objects started to fly throughout the residence and hit the ones present. The 4 exorcism durations of the house did no longer yield any consequences.

In desperation, the family have grow to be to a medium.

Milton Keynes UK
Ingram Content Group UK Ltd.
UKHW020636161123
432684UK00016B/504